Dawn,

You are a Rock star.

♡,

Jenn T. Grace

PRAISE FOR BEYOND THE RAINBOW

"Authenticity and personal inspiration are central to every lesson Jenn teaches—especially in *Beyond the Rainbow*. By exploring years of experience as a highly-respected expert in diversity marketing and business development, Jenn has crafted an essential guide that can help everyone, from startup to C-Suite, achieve success with the LGBTQ market."

- Justin Nelson, Co-Founder & President, National Gay & Lesbian Chamber of Commerce (NGLCC)

"If your company wants to reach the LGBTQ community, you need a strategy. *Beyond the Rainbow* provides a smart and nuanced framework to help you reach this powerful and lucrative market."

- Dorie Clark, Author of Reinventing You and Stand Out, and Adjunct Professor, Duke University's Fuqua School of Business

"Jenn has done it again! As a business owner and ally, I found *Beyond the Rainbow* packed with straightforward advice and guidance for my employees and me in the post-Orlando/post-Obama, challenging new world. We'll be stepping up our commitment to support equality and serve as a safe place for the LGBTQ community."

- Louise Albin, Owner of Cafe Louise Catering

∽

"We live in a world that's driven by analytics, statistics and tangible results, however does that truly measure a strong culture and an accepted workforce? Simply meeting quotas and providing benefits is not enough in today's workforce to attract and retain top LGBTQ talent. *Beyond the Rainbow* is the conductor in the symphony of business to help organizations understand that diversity is simply inviting people to the party. To truly differentiate yourself from the masses by creating a strong value proposition, you must create the song that asks your workforce to dance."

- Sara Donnan McCook, Global Ops, Strategy &
Design Program Manager at United Airlines, and
Founder of & cake. Bold Personal Brand Innovation.

∽

"*Beyond the Rainbow* is a must-read for everyone who wants to learn the best practices in LGBTQ marketing. Jenn has an amazing knack for using personal stories to relate everything from the basics to in-depth practical advice. After nearly 30 years in the business world, even this old dog learned a few new tricks from Jenn's insightful ideas! Whether you're an outsider looking in or an insider looking out for everyone around you, everyone can relate to Jenn's stories and find some actionable 'I can do this, too' tips."

- Branan Cooper, Fortune 500 Financial
Executive and Public Speaker

∽

"Leaders will find value in *Beyond the Rainbow*. Jenn helps leaders, whether fresh in the position or those that have led for decades, understand the importance of inclusion within the workplace, specifically within the LGBTQ community. As a leader, it is not your job to understand what it's like to be LGBTQ, rather how you can be an effective ally, and create a safe work environment. Jenn helps you understand the importance of allyship and lets you empathize with a community that some fear only due to their ignorance. A must read within today's business and political environment. This is not a topic that will disappear, but rather a topic that will affect your business more so now than ever before. Just remember that the 'why' should never be about the almighty buck. Jenn helps you understand the 'why' as well."

- Robert Beaven, Founder and CEO
of The Haddow Group

"*Beyond the Rainbow* provides whip-smart but common sense strategies towards LGBTQ inclusion in a very approachable way. There's something for everyone in this book (even those of us who are LGBTQ)! Jenn's stories are relatable to all of us and provide insights that guide us towards authentically serving LGBTQ consumers."

- *Bernadette Smith, Equality Institute*

∾

"Jenn is transparent and authentic in bringing her own experiences to life in a way that should cause us all to examine the kind of environment we play a part in creating in our own workplaces. Today's employees are looking for organizations whose values match their own. As a result, it is critically important for organizations to turn the mirror on themselves and challenge their internal practices, not just their external actions, in order to attract today's workforce and customer base. The concepts in *Beyond the Rainbow* are simple and easy to understand even for those who do not have a great deal of familiarity with the LGBTQ community. It offers 'doable' solutions that companies and individuals can use to fight hate and discrimination in their day-to-day operations. This is an important guidebook!"

- *Joelle A. Murchison, Diversity and Inclusion Champion*

"As a professional who always looks at markets that could be a good fit for my service offering, I was excited to read this book. After reading *Beyond the Rainbow*, I felt prepared to put together a marketing strategy that would be well received by the LGBTQ community. But perhaps more importantly, I understood the importance of preparing for this outreach. Just because you are open to LGBTQ issues or the community, doesn't prepare you to do business in that space. Don't even think about launching a LGBTQ marketing campaign without reading this book!"

- Monika D'Agostino, Owner,
Consultative Sales Academy

✌

"*Beyond the Rainbow* shares critically important professional and personal knowledge of the LGBTQ community that reaches beyond the community itself and into the lives of allies and business leaders, and their circles of influence. The guidance, insights and resources Jenn shares enables professional leaders and allies to the LGBTQ community to understand how important it is that everyone bring their whole selves to work. A must read for anyone looking to positively impact the business or workplace around them."

- Dave Ciliberto, Adjunct Instructor
at Cornell University

"A great read to better understand, manage and lead the change needed for an inclusive and diverse society and workplace. Through her personal stories, Jenn provides insights into the struggles of the LGBTQ community. This glimpse is all one needs to begin to understand (or help others learn) the challenges LGBTQ people face in today's society and that transcend to the workplace. The stories shared could easily translate to personal experiences of other diverse groups, which makes *Beyond the Rainbow* a great resource to help promote the change needed so that all individuals can have equal opportunity, easily and comfortably live, and bring their whole self to work."

- Wanda L. Ramos, Human Resources Professional

"Anyone who has been to a PFLAG meeting knows that it is not just LGBTQ folks who pay close attention to how companies reach out to the LGBTQ market. Families and allies also support organizations that engage with the community and respect their LGBTQ employees. In *Beyond the Rainbow*, Jenn guides you through the 'whys' and 'hows' of connecting with the LGBTQ market. Her personal stories, marketing expertise, and frank talk combine perfectly to help re-frame your thinking—so that your company may become a true ally of the community."

- Lori Davison, President of PFLAG Hartford

"Jenn has dedicated herself to the work of demystifying the "otherness" of the LGBTQ community, and to creating a path toward understanding and collaboration. With straightforward language, real stories and a heart whose compass is always seeking true inclusion, she helps us translate and transport across the things, which divide us. Her fresh and frank approach illuminates differences in a way that helps us feel more confident in how to move forward, and opens the door to meaningful change. Her book will help educate and enable lasting engagement with this valuable market segment and vibrant community, and empower simple human connections. Her insights and experience have helped to make me a more powerful ally to the LGBTQ community. And have shown me that there is still more I can do."

- Nancy Mace, Mace & Associates

୶

"Addressing the needs of the LGBTQ community is not only the right thing to do, it is a necessary step in creating business success and economic opportunities in all organizations. In this wonderful book, Jenn helps the reader understand her 'Inclusion Based Marketing' approach. Lending a voice to a community that has long been ignored and marginalized, she makes a convincing case for addressing a market segment, which had a whopping $917 billion dollars in buying power in 2016. *Beyond the Rainbow*, a reflection of her extensive experience, provides the reader with a roadmap needed to succeed in this market. I was particularly impressed with her honesty and sincere approach to addressing commonly held fears and prejudices. Her clear and succinct writing make her book a pleasure to read. There are so many 'ah-hahs!' in this book that makes it hard to put it down."

- Maria Valentin, Vice President,
Strategic Markets (retired in 2016),
First American Title Insurance Company

∽

"No one is more equipped to help you embrace the LGBTQ community than Jenn T. Grace. Read *Beyond the Rainbow* for practical advice and personal stories on how to create a welcoming working environment for everyone."

- Brian Honigman, Adjunct Professor
at NYU and Marketing Consultant

∽

"Jenn is a powerful catalyst for inspiring workplaces to go beyond dusty LGBTQ marketing campaigns. Her wisdom and passion motivates business leaders to step into their power as change agents capable of explaining why connecting with LGBTQ communities is essential. With an open mind, you too will gain the confidence and strategies necessary to transform your workplace into one fit for the 21st Century."

- Rhodes Perry, Founder and Host
of The Out Entrepreneur, LLC

"*Beyond the Rainbow* is magnificently heartfelt, truthful and emotionally honest. Jenn brilliantly guides the reader through the important steps on why it is so important to be an ally to the LGBTQ community and how to properly communicate with your LGBTQ colleagues and customers. She does justice to a critically important yet delicate topic and provides eye-opening insight into her own experience. I have a new level of empathy for what it means to be an ally and a deeper desire to be part of the solution for change. Beyond practical marketing advice, *Beyond the Rainbow* is a must-read for anyone with a heart and a desire to be a better more open minded human being."

- Stacy Garcia, Founder and CEO of Stacy Garcia Design House and Publisher of Life-Styled.net

"Jenn delivers an important and inspiring message with honesty, clarity and openness. Her boots-on-the-ground advice for why and how to effectively reach and support the LGBTQ market will help any company tailor their marketing efforts. Jenn teaches by showing, not just telling. *Beyond the Rainbow* should be part of every employee handbook!"

- Lisa Corrado, Motivational Storyteller and Coach, Creator of The Felix Culpa Project

"*Beyond the Rainbow* is filled with honest, no-nonsense wisdom that will make me better at promoting LGBTQ people, causes and initiatives. Jenn has a knack for helping individuals and businesses up their game. I am grateful for this new resource that will allow me to do just that."

- Cindi Creager, Co-Founder CreagerCole Communications LLC

❧

"This book makes the strong case that marketing to the LGBTQ community—and aligning your employees behind that effort—will pay enormous dividends. Jenn clearly lays out the rationale for approaching this lucrative market, and the steps every organization can take to ensure this approach is done authentically, respectfully, and strategically. Don't miss this critical resource!"

- Jennifer Brown, CEO, Jennifer Brown Consulting

❧

"When it comes to business information relating to the LGBTQ community my first stop is always Jenn—a book, podcast or in a conversation, she never disappoints. Jenn is a passionate, authentic, and a vulnerable writer who puts her experiences out there to ensure we are all more educated and aware. *Beyond the Rainbow* is no different. I know it will be a resource I will reference and share for years to come."

- Kristen Hickey, Corporate Social Responsibility Expert

"Jenn provides a valuable look at the assimilation of the LGBTQ community into the workforce and our communities. American businesses are targeting diverse groups like never before largely because of the economic impact. With nearly $1 trillion in buying power, the LGBTQ community rivals other diverse groups and Jenn showcases how businesses of any size can properly embrace the LGBTQ community. *Beyond the Rainbow* is a powerful book."

> *- Jeff Berger, Founder & CEO National Association of*
> *Gay & Lesbian Real Estate Professionals (NAGLREP)*

"As a diversity and inclusion consultant and a proud LGBTQ ally, I have never been so inspired to help this community more and now feel like I have the tools to do so after reading *Beyond the Rainbow*. I felt myself on the edge of my seat wanting to get up immediately and do everything that I can to help members of the LGBTQ community feel more comfortable bringing their full selves to work and life, and at the same time slowing down my pace to make sure that I was carefully reading every sentence to ensure that my approach would be carefully executed. Thank you for writing this very important masterpiece, Jenn!"

> *- Colleen Cassidy Bastian, Ph.D, PCC,*
> *Diversity & Inclusion Consultant &*
> *Executive Coach, Cassidy Consulting LLC*

BEYOND THE RAINBOW

BEYOND THE RAINBOW

*Personal Stories and Practical Strategies
to Help your Business & Workplace
Connect with the LGBTQ Market*

JENN T. GRACE

PURPOSE
DRIVEN
PUBLISHING

For permission requests, write to the publisher, addressed "Attention: Permissions Coordinator," at the address below.

Purpose Driven Publishing
141 Weston Street, #155
Hartford, CT, 06141

PURPOSE
DRIVEN
PUBLISHING

The opinions expressed by the Author are not necessarily those held by Purpose Driven Publishing.

Ordering Information: Quantity sales and special discounts are available on quantity purchases by corporations, associations, and others. For details, contact the publisher at the address above.

Edited by: Heather B. Habelka
Cover design by: Valerie Gyorgy

Printed in the United States of America.

ISBN-13: 978-1-946384-05-8
ISBN-10: 1-946384-05-4
Library of Congress Control Number: 2017937189

First edition, June 2017.

The information contained within this book is strictly for informational purposes. The material may include information, products, or services by third parties. As such, the Author and Publisher do not assume responsibility or liability for any third party material or opinions. Readers are advised to do their own due diligence when it comes to making decisions.

Purpose Driven Publishing works with authors, and aspiring authors, who have a story to tell and a brand to build. Do you have a book idea you would like us to consider publishing? Please visit PurposeDrivenPublishing.com for more information.

DEDICATION

This book is dedicated to every brave individual who has encountered discrimination and hate in their lifetime.

And to the 49 lives lost at Pulse Nightclub on June 12, 2016 in Orlando—you will not be forgotten.

Akyra Monet Murray, 18
Jason Benjamin Josaphat, 19
Luis Omar Ocasio-Capo, 20
Alejandro Barrios Martinez, 21
Cory James Connell, 21
Juan Ramon Guerrero, 22
Luis S. Vielma, 22
Peter O. Gonzalez-Cruz, 22
Stanley Almodovar III, 23
Christopher Joseph Sanfeliz, 24
Jonathan Antonio Camuy Vega, 24
Yilmary Rodriguez Solivan, 24
Amanda Alvear, 25
Anthony Luis Laureano Disla, 25
Enrique L. Rios Jr., 25

Geraldo A. Ortiz-Jimenez, 25

Gilberto Ramon Silva Menendez, 25

Juan Chevez-Martinez, 25

Leroy Valentin Fernandez, 25

Tevin Eugene Crosby, 25

Mercedez Marisol Flores, 26

Oscar A Aracena-Montero, 26

Frank Hernandez Escalante, 27

Jean C. Nives Rodriguez, 27

Angel L. Candelario-Padro, 28

Antonio Davon Brown, 29

Darryl Roman Burt II, 29

Eddie Jamoldroy Justice, 30

Miguel Angel Honorato, 30

Jerald Arthur Wright, 31

Simon Adrian Carrillo Fernandez, 31

Christopher "Drew" Leinonen, 32

Deonka Deidra Drayton, 32

Joel Rayon Paniagua, 32

Martin Benitez Torres, 33

Rodolfo Ayala-Ayala, 33

Shane Evan Tomlinson, 33

Edward Sotomayor Jr., 34

Jean Carlos Mendez Perez, 35

Xavier Emmanuel Serrano Rosado, 35

Eric Ivan Ortiz-Rivera, 36

Juan P. Rivera Velazquez, 37

K.J. Morris, 37

Luis Daniel Wilson-Leon, 37

Luis Daniel Conde, 39

Javier Jorge-Reyes, 40

Paul Terrell Henry, 41

Brenda Lee Marquez McCool, 49

Franky Jimmy Dejesus Velazquez, 50

- -

I am human, I am love

And my heart beats in my blood

Love will always win

Underneath the skin

Everybody's got a pulse

- *Melissa Etheridge, "Pulse"*

- -

ACKNOWLEDGEMENTS

This book is a combination of over 10 years of friendships, partnerships, relationships and conversations that have changed as the LGBTQ landscape has changed. If it were not for the amazingly wise people around me this book would not exist.

I thank the readers of my blog and the listeners of my podcast—you are always inspiring me by asking insightful questions and patiently waiting for guidance in return. I thank every person who has commented on an article or left a message on social media—your feedback, good, bad and sometimes ugly, is what continues to help shape the conversation around LGBTQ equality in the workplace and in the world of entrepreneurship. Keep being a vocal champion for what you believe in—this is what makes our world go round.

I thank my clients for their partnerships over the years. From the Fortune 100s who are at the forefront of LGBTQ equality to the Fortune 1000s who are striving to get from behind the pack, you inspire, and challenge, me every day. To the internal champions within these organizations who have the determination and conviction to see their LGBTQ efforts through to fruition—it is sometimes your lone voice that impacts an employee base of tens of thousands—your bravery to stand up for what is right is awe inspiring. I'm honored to work with you—to call you clients, and to call you friends.

I thank the truly gifted people who are constantly pushing me outside of my comfort zone, whether I want to go there or not! To Maria, my coach and mentor, thank you for being with me from the very start, and for guiding me every step of the way. To the people in my mastermind groups—it is because of your behind-the-scenes wisdom and support that I'm able to better serve my audience.

I thank my best friends. Virginia, it is your ongoing commitment to treating your LGBTQ patients properly that led me to start my blog so many years ago. Your bravery to ask the questions others wouldn't has truly impacted tens of thousands. Niki, your guidance, both personally and professionally, has been unmatched. Your constant support and friendship through all of the ups and downs doesn't go unnoticed.

To everyone who was a part of the creation of this book, I am forever grateful for your contributions. To my editor, and friend, Heather—you took this book from good to great and I know the readers have you to thank in large part.

I thank the National Gay & Lesbian Chamber of Commerce for opening my eyes in 2006 to the LGBTQ business equality movement. Had I not found your organization I would not be where I am today. And to all of the other LGBTQ advocacy organizations bravely dedicated to change—I thank you for what you do.

And finally, I thank my wife Andrea. She is my rock, the center of my universe, the force within my life that keeps our family and household on track, which allows me to pursue my passion for advocating on behalf of our community.

TABLE OF CONTENTS

NANCY WYMAN, LIEUTENANT GOVERNOR OF CONNECTICUT

In April 1991, when I was in my second term at the Connecticut General Assembly, Speaker Richard Balducci opened discussion on one of the most meaningful votes I would make during my tenure as a state representative. It was a bill that would expand our equal opportunity laws and thereby protect lesbian, gay, and bisexual people from discrimination in Connecticut.

From my desk on the floor of the State House of Representatives, I could see the hundreds of citizens who had packed themselves into the small gallery over the Speaker's dais. For over a decade, those residents had come by the thousands to rallies and public hearings. They had written countless letters; made innumerable phone calls, and took every opportunity to meet with their legislators. They had laid it all on the line for this vote, telling us their personal stories of what discrimination looked like in their jobs and communities.

Hours of debate ensued, but finally, the old vote tally machine dinged to a close and the House Clerk announced passage of this historic legislation. Amid cheering and celebrating, Connecticut became one of a handful of states in the nation to explicitly protect our LGB residents. We had done the right thing.

We had more work to do.

Connecticut would go on to be among the first in the country to pass co-parent adoption protections, provide for civil union, codify same-sex marriage, and ensure transgender residents were added to our anti-discrimination laws. We instituted a ban on state-funded travel to states that were eroding equal protection laws and legalizing business practices that discriminated against LGBTQ residents.

In *Beyond the Rainbow*, Jenn asks us to consider the obstacles that LGBTQ citizens hurdle every day. From recognizing the implications of being "out" at work, to creating inclusive marketing campaigns, there are ways that every business can mitigate the obstacles and show their support for LGBTQ employees and customers.

But Jenn's book goes a step further in challenging our own understanding of bias. She urges her readers to reflect on 'why'—because intention is key, and so are ethics and integrity.

Her drive to suss out purpose offers a valuable lesson to the business community—not just how do you reach the LGBTQ market, but how do you invest in the LGBTQ community as a whole, because by buying your products, choosing your service, eating at your restaurants, or staying at your hotels, the LGBTQ community is investing in you.

Beyond the Rainbow starts conversations and identifies the ways we can better understand each other as consumers, neighbors, and humans seeking a good life.

One last thing. Not even a week after we passed the anti-discrimination bill, my daughter, home for the summer from college, was denied an apartment rental because the landlord thought she and her roommate were lesbians.

"We just passed a bill a week ago that prevents you from discriminating against lesbians …" I began the conversation with the landlord. She got the apartment, but the broader point was made: passing this law wasn't about protecting "other" people, it was about protecting all people.

In this political climate, there is no more important time for the business community to be an active ally and pursue a culture of inclusion for LGBTQ residents.

Nancy Wyman

PREFACE

I began writing this book before the results of the 2016 U.S. Presidential election. On November 9, 2016, the LGBTQ (lesbian, gay, bisexual, transgender and queer) world shifted. Your world may have shifted too, perhaps for different reasons. As a result of this shift, this book is different. It isn't gentle. Why? Because now, in this highly-charged political climate, the LGBTQ community needs you.

We need more options when choosing who to do business with, and who to work for. We are tired of discrimination that is riddled with judgment and fear.

I believe social change happens first in business—possibly in *your* business or workplace. To affect change you must come from a place of knowledge, compassion, and confidence. This book *will* provide you with the strategies and resources you'll need to positively impact the LGBTQ community around you. This book *will* show you how to stretch your empathetic muscle, which will result in a better world for LGBTQ people to work in, *and* in genuine business opportunities for you.

The market potential of the LGBTQ community is immense. There is more opportunity than there are people to serve it. The landscape is ripe for the picking, but you need to understand the community first. The LGBTQ community is riddled with baggage—yes, I said it. You must know how to navigate that baggage effectively, and sensitively.

As a result of reading this book, and with the intention of authentically implementing the strategies outlined here, you will be equipped to be a business the LGBTQ community wants to work for, and do business with. You will understand the community in a way that your competition does not. This is a big deal. Pun intended.

A portion of the profit from this book will be dedicated to ending LGBTQ discrimination.

CHAPTER 1

MY FIRST 'PROFESSIONAL' JOB

I N 2004, WHEN I graduated college with a degree in communications, I headed west to Connecticut with my girlfriend at the time. As I prepared to move from Boston's North Shore, I had big dreams of making a name for myself in advertising, specifically in the beverage industry. Fairfield County, which borders New York, was where all of the ad agencies were at the time. It was a bit of a commute, but I pounded the pavement daily searching for any position that would get my foot in the door of the advertising world. I naively thought I was going to get right into advertising and break free of retail. This was not the case—as many recent college graduates quickly come to learn.

So I began applying for jobs where I could get office experience. Up to this point I had held many different types of retail jobs, so I began looking for office jobs in customer service.

Much to my surprise, I found an office job at an insurance company within a couple of months. Living in the Hartford area it is a rite of passage to work in insurance at one point or another in your career!

On my first day of work, I falsely assumed if I could thrive on a factory floor where I was one of four women in a factory full of hundreds of men—and start a landscaping company at age 17—I could do anything!

I was wrong.

During my job search I had applied for at least 100 customer service positions. When I submitted my resume to this one particular insurance company, it caught the attention of the CEO who was actively seeking marketing help. As a smaller family owned insurance company with about 100 employees, they didn't have a formal marketing department. The task of marketing fell on product development and sales. It was a pivotal time in the growth of this company, and the CEO was looking to build a marketing department.

I had a meeting with the CEO and I walked away *so* excited for the possibilities. When he made the formal job offer, I said a big hell yes!

My first week I was bright eyed and bushy tailed—I felt free! "To hell with retail, I was finally an adult embarking on my career!"

I fell in love at this job. Her name? Marketing. Every day was different in this job and everything was new. I assisted the sales team, created newsletters and wrote copy for the website. I dove in head first to get every job done. I was in *love.* I had the flexibility to learn on the job as I went, without the fear of repercussions if I royally screwed something up—which certainly happened more than once! (If we meet in person, ask me about the "Clock Fiasco of 2008").

Blissfully entering this new type of environment I looked forward to what I would learn the next day. For the first couple of weeks I kept my head down and was laser focused on getting my job done. I didn't spend much time socializing. Since marketing was a new department, I was put in the back of the building with the sales team and the person who worked in product development. It was quiet back there, which meant I was able to get a lot of my work done without distractions. This was still such a foreign concept to me, as I was accustomed to the hustle and bustle of retail. To work in silence, on the project at hand, took some time to get used to.

It wasn't long before I became friendly with the person I shared a cubicle wall with. We became fast friends. But not before I was confronted with an incredibly uncomfortable situation.

The First Time I "Covered" Up

One day, my co-worker made an assumption that I had a boyfriend. I had only been on the job for a couple of weeks and our conversations had consisted primarily of small talk. Just before I moved to Connecticut my girlfriend and I had gotten engaged, so I was wearing an engagement ring. My new friend assumed I was engaged to a man.

When my new friend made the assumption that I had a boyfriend, I didn't correct her.

This was the *very first* time I "covered" my identity. "Covering" is essentially when you hide some aspect of your identity for fear of political or social consequences. People can cover their political views, religious beliefs, a disability, being LGBTQ, being a single parent and so on. When we reveal certain aspects of who we are, it can prompt unwarranted comments and outright discrimination. Many people walk a fine line in revealing who they are when making new friends, especially at work.

For me, in that instant, I chose not to correct her. If I had to guess, I'd bet you've covered your identity at least once in your life. When you are LGBTQ, covering can be a significant part of your daily life. Covering feels like fight or flight—it's an instantaneous decision that has a significant impact. You either hypothetically fight—by coming out as LGBTQ, or take flight—by skirting the question or statement by covering or ignoring it altogether.

I encourage you to reach out to an LGBTQ person in your life, someone you are close to, and ask them about an experience when they covered their identity. I'm certain they will have a story to share with you. Trust me, it'll be an eye opening conversation, especially if you are part of their story!

In that split second, when my co-worker assumed I had a boyfriend, I didn't correct her. It was the first time anything about my relationship came up in conversation. I froze.

What I did instead was engage in what is known as the pronoun game. This is done by avoiding the use of gender-specific pronouns in an effort to conceal your relationship with someone of the same sex. Rather than saying 'she,' I switched things up to say 'us,' 'we,' 'they,' etc. It's a way of avoiding having to 'come out' as LGBTQ to someone, without feeling like you are bold-faced lying.

What happens next is that you cross, what I call, an invisible threshold. Nothing good usually follows from here—until, and if, you are ready to right the wrong. This can be an uncomfortable and stressful situation.

My girlfriend at the time had a gender-neutral name, which did come in handy. This allowed me to use her real name without directly outing myself. However, the constant use of someone's first name starts to sound awkward and suspicious. For example, if a co-worker asked me what

> What I did instead was engage in what is known as the pronoun game. This is done by avoiding the use of gender-specific pronouns in an effort to conceal your relationship with someone of the same sex. Rather than saying 'she,' I switched things up to say 'us,' 'we,' 'they,' etc. It's a way of avoiding having to 'come out' as LGBTQ to someone, without feeling like you are boldfaced lying.

'Jamie' and I did over the weekend, and if I was able to use the pronoun she or her, our conversation would flow smoothly. But to respond with only a first name gets awkward—fast. "First we went to dinner, then a movie. Then Jamie [she] surprised me with a trip to the beach. Jamie [she] is so thoughtful."

Hearing the name Jamie, Jamie, Jamie over and over again sounds strange. While the person on the receiving end of this conversation may not get what you are doing, they will definitely pick up that something seems odd.

An LGBTQ person who is struggling with this is not looking to intentionally hurt you—they are doing it to protect themselves in an unknown environment. A person's demeanor and their actions can turn on a dime the moment they learn you are

LGBTQ. Coming out can be a very dangerous situation in many parts of the world.

Please don't take it personally if you find yourself on the receiving end of a situation like this. I encourage you to put yourself in the shoes of an LGBTQ person for just a moment to see how it might feel, having to assess the dangers around you before being able to reveal your true identity.

In my case, our friendship developed very quickly and yet I was still hiding something huge about my life. It was at least a month before I finally got up the nerve to come out to her. It was hard.

I knew that my being a lesbian and engaged to a woman was not going to impact her in any way whatsoever. But what I worried about was hurting her feelings. For her thinking I didn't trust her to tell her sooner. I wrestled with how to tell her and then just one day I did. She was caught by surprise, but we laughed about it, and we moved on.

Fortunately for both of us, I came out, she understood and for the past 13 years we have remained close friends.

Your Voice Matters

This situation turned out okay for me, but this is *not* the case for countless other LGBTQ people who find themselves in similar situations. Not everyone is fortunate enough to have understanding colleagues or co-workers. This is where you come in.

As a result of reading this book you will be equipped to be an ally; a straight person who supports equality for members of the

LGBTQ community and serves as a safe space the LGBTQ community can come to.

In the vein of knowledge, it is important for you to understand that in 28 states in the United States it is perfectly legal to be fired from your job for being lesbian, gay or bisexual. In 32 states you can legally be fired for being transgender.[1] Now that marriage equality is the law of the land in all 50 states, an LGBTQ couple can be married on a Saturday, and in 28 of them be fired from their job on a Monday, simply because they got married over the weekend. More than half of the LGBTQ population in the United States is living in states where this scenario can and does play out on a regular basis.

In the 22 states that do have some form of legal protections, these protections are on a state, not federal level. For example, as a resident of Connecticut, there are state laws that protect LGBTQ people from being wrongly fired from their jobs. However, this *does not* hold true for Tennessee, for example. If my wife and I decided to relocate to Nashville, she could be fired from her job as a teacher without cause. This would be perfectly legal under Tennessee state law. She would not be protected by the federal government.

The brutal reality is that many people, LGBTQ or otherwise, live in certain geographic areas for their job, to be close to their family, because they cannot afford to move elsewhere, or because they don't want to start their lives over. I just happened to be born, raised and have lived my entire life in New England. When I hear a colleague talk about being fired from her NCAA

---

1 http://www.lgbtmap.org/equality-maps/non_discrimination_laws

coaching position at the college she worked for, after they found out she was a lesbian, it breaks my heart. The knee jerk reaction when you hear these stories is to say, "Well, Michelle, why don't you move to a state that protects you?" That is so much easier said than done.

Because LGBTQ people comprise only 4.1% of the adult population in the U.S. being the only LGBTQ person in the room is *very* common.

This is why your opinion matters and your voice counts. As an entrepreneur, an employer or a corporate professional, you have the opportunity to advocate on behalf of the LGBTQ community in a way to help gain these protections for all people.

Businesses and corporations set their own standards. So while you might own a business in Arkansas that doesn't have statewide workplace protections in place, you, as a business owner or a human resources professional have the power to establish workplace protections that protect *your* employees, even in states where it is legal to fire someone because they are LGBTQ.[2]

> Because LGBTQ people comprise only 4.1% of the adult population in the U.S. being the only LGBTQ person in the room is *very* common.

My mantra is '*Change Happens in Business.*' Businesses have the complete power to make change even in political climates that may not be overly conducive to do so. Later on, I will share details of a Fortune 100 company I worked with to implement

---

2 http://www.gallup.com/poll/201731/lgbt-identification-rises.aspx

policies that protect their LGBTQ workforce and attract top talent. Working to make social change in business is not only good for the bottom line, it is becoming the gold standard for organizations across the globe.

There are many studies available that show happier employees make more productive employees. It has been shown time and time again that when an LGBTQ employee can bring their whole self to their jobs and their workplace, they contribute more and produce better results.

You may wonder how that is.

Let's go back to my personal story—it took me about a month before I felt comfortable enough to share my true identity with one co-worker—one person—one out of my 100 colleagues.

In the month leading up to outing myself to her I was obsessed with it. As soon as I crossed that invisible threshold and began lying by omission I was preoccupied. I loved my job, but I was equally caught in that feeling of fight or flight. I was focused on when the perfect time would present itself, when I could casually slip it into conversation. I wondered how she was going to react. Was she going to out me to the rest of the company? These thoughts, and fears were constantly on my mind, when I should have been focused on my job performance.

This is the experience of LGBTQ people everywhere, every day. Even in states such as Connecticut, where it is illegal to fire someone because they are LGBTQ, it does not take away that imminent fear an LGBTQ person might have of how their coworkers will react. Someone may be working for a company that is pro-LGBTQ, with all of the workplace policies and protections in place, but their immediate manager may be homophobic.

Company policies can protect an employee to a certain degree, but it won't stop the subtle or inadvertent harassment someone might face on a day-to-day basis. This is what LGBTQ people fear—and sadly, this is the reality for many.

Therefore, it is easier to engage in the pronoun game and to lie by omission in order to protect your identity, yourself and your job.

Think about the un-calculated amount of energy that goes into hiding your identity while on the job. For me, I used precious energy and mental bandwidth hiding my personal relationship rather than focusing on my job, a job I genuinely loved.

The LGBTQ Community is Watching

Your LGBTQ colleagues, co-workers or employees are vigilant— they are on high alert for perceived threats. They are listening and paying close attention to conversations and reactions where anything LGBTQ comes up. As small as the interaction may be, they are watching you and making decisions in that moment of whether or not it is safe to reveal their identities.

There is another side to my story, one that I learned much later. I had an uneasy feeling from my first day on the job. I wasn't able to put my finger on it, but it was there, and that alone is enough for most LGBTQ people to put their guard up, which may have been part of the reason I was reluctant to come out at first.

I eventually heard through the rumor mill that within a few days of starting my job, speculation began about me. My boss was overheard stating that I had the 'captain of the softball team lesbian look' about me.

Growing up I was an athlete but post-high school I began to cover that part of my identity. I did not want people to stereotype me in the exact way that my boss had. In this particular instance, at age 23, hearing this was how I was viewed made me shove that aspect of my identity even further into the past.

Your words impact LGBTQ people in a way that you may have never realized. It is my hope that this book will equip you with the awareness, and knowledge, to draw on in situations where you can positively impact the lives of LGBTQ people around you.

It didn't take long before my work environment became toxic. Like most workplaces, my company had a large number of people who thrived on spreading gossip and being involved in other people's drama. Because of my somewhat aloof attitude, I had surface relationships with the people at the core of the gossip and drama. I didn't want to be an outright bitch, but I also didn't want them to think that it was okay to share people's business with me. I surely wasn't going to share any of my business with them!

> Your words impact LGBTQ people in a way that you may have never realized.

So instead of hearing the nasty comments directly from them, I would overhear things in passing, like the time I heard a claims representative comment that the customer on the phone sounded like a 'faggot' or the time someone from accounting said a co-worker looked like a dyke. My workplace began to feel dangerous. I knew *no one* else could know anything about me.

This was uncharted territory for me. In my eight years of working in retail I had never, ever heard such hateful things directed toward LGBTQ people.

The striking contrast of being free and open to being thrust into a gossip filled workplace where talking behind people's backs and being cruel to one another was the norm, felt so foreign to me. This was not what I had in mind when I left retail to pursue a 'professional' office job. But, it was this experience that has led me to exactly where I am today, so while this might sound strange, I will forever be grateful for this first-hand journey in workplace discrimination.

Vodka & My $1 Million Idea

In the summer of 2006, after two years working at the insurance company, I hit a breaking point and requested a meeting with the CEO. I anxiously explained that while I truly loved my job and was grateful for the opportunity, I had to resign. He was surprised and shocked, but his response equally caught me off guard. He point blank asked what he could do to keep me around. I was 25 and hadn't fully thought this through. At this point in my life I had started and ended many jobs—usually when you say you resign or quit, you give your two weeks notice and you move on. But this was different.

During this meeting I did not tell him why I was unhappy. I was only 25 and honestly, I was scared to tell him that his company was filled with bigotry and hate. To stop me from quitting he suggested that I take on a special project, a $1 million project. This project would be something that I'd work on to make me happy, but would also impact the bottom line of the business. I was not expecting this. My desk was already packed up and I was prepared to be escorted out of the building!

I left the meeting in shock. I had gone in to quit my job, but I walked away with an opportunity to be happier and make a difference for the company. At the time it felt like he understood me. I felt optimistic and cared for. I went back to my desk feeling inspired. Looking back on this situation now, it was a brilliant move on the CEO's part to keep a talented person on the job!

I mulled over his proposition, trying to generate an idea that would distract me from the drama and generate an additional $1 million in revenue.

And then, an image of an Absolut Vodka bottle flashed before my eyes.

Eureka!

Let's market to the LGBTQ community!

My original dream had been to move to Connecticut to work for an advertising agency that served the beverage industry. My interest began when I started collecting and analyzing alcohol ads from magazines. I was fascinated by how well the industry knew their market and target customers. I began collecting these ads in 1998 and to this day, nearly 20 years later, it is still a hobby of mine.

My eureka moment popped when I saw an ad for Absolut Vodka. The bottle was wrapped in the rainbow. It clearly was designed to connect directly with the LGBTQ community.

In 2007, LGBTQ advertising was *far* less than it is now, and honestly, I didn't really know there was actual strategy behind any of it. In my mind it seemed like a great idea, but I hadn't the slightest clue of where to start.

My Double Life

I met with the CEO six months after that original meeting. I was nervous as hell! I had spent months preparing my case. I was prepared to sell him on why marketing to the LGBTQ community was something worthy of investing in, and why I was a natural fit to spearhead the effort. Much to my surprise, he gave me carte blanche.

In addition to outing my idea, I also outed myself at this meeting. I shared with him that I had heard less than ideal water cooler conversations, where the words dyke and faggot were used. I was frustrated and hurt, but I sincerely wanted to make a change in my workspace, even though at the time I had no idea how I would actually do it.

This was uncharted territory, in more ways than one!

I spent several months soaking up every bit of information that would help me reach the LGBTQ community. My goal was two-fold, to provide our customers with a safe experience and to add a significant amount of additional revenue to the company's bottom line.

Since I was laser focused on my research, I had been turning a blind eye to the hateful remarks I would hear either directed toward me or anyone else at work. When I began this LGBTQ marketing project and people in the company caught wind of it, I essentially outed myself. Ironically, I was still in protective mode, despite the fact that I was working on such a visibly 'out' project.

This project gave me the opportunity to connect with amazing people outside of the office. I traveled across the country to attend conferences and to meet with the LGBTQ agents who were selling our insurance. I wanted everyone I came in contact with to be aware of the good work we were doing in support of our LGBTQ customers and agents.

I was filled with hope and inspiration. I would return to the office with a notebook full of ideas and boundless energy. I was hell bent on generating $1 million by connecting with the LGBTQ market.

The trifecta of doing good for the LGBTQ community as a whole, while affecting change in Corporate America, combined with generating revenue seemed too good to be true!

I knew I had found my calling, even if I couldn't put my finger on it…yet!

But returning to my office felt like having a bucket of ice water thrown in my face.

I would be in the office for less than a day before some derogatory remark would be thrown my way. At this point I was the LGBTQ poster child in the company, which made me outwardly hated by those who weren't so accepting and tolerant. Despite my environment, I did the best I could to keep my head down and do my job.

I spent over two years working on this project, but the day came when I simply couldn't do it anymore. I couldn't live two lives. I was out of the office, speaking with the LGBTQ community, proclaiming we were *the* company to work with if you are LGBTQ. But then I'd walk into the office to overhear someone calling me a dyke. I'd had enough.

I hit my breaking point when I came to the realization that I was living a double life. I could no longer reconcile what I was saying publicly with what was happening to me at the office. I was committed to serving all of our customers, but I had been specifically responsible for our LGBTQ customers. I was responsible for their safety. I had promised that they would be cared for, and yet I lived in constant fear that a customer would hear their claims rep call them a faggot.

> I could no longer reconcile what I was saying publicly with what was happening to me at the office.

To this day, I don't directly fault the CEO for my experience, but I do fault him for not putting higher standards and policies in place to stop the bigotry and hatred among his employees.

I learned a very valuable lesson that I continue to teach my clients over a decade later: If you want to market to the LGBTQ community, you *must* have internal policies in place that protect your LGBTQ employees and customers. Any customer-facing employee must be properly trained on how to communicate with the LGBTQ community in an appropriate and pleasant manner. If you skip this step, I promise you, you are wasting time and money. You won't see one dollar in your return on investment.

The biggest lesson here is—this entire situation could have been avoided. The entire thing.

CHAPTER 2

CONNECTING WITH
YOUR COMMUNITY

FROM CORPORATE AMERICA to Main Street America the experiences I described in the previous chapter are *very* common. Homophobia and discrimination in the workplace are widespread issues that are taking a long time to solve, despite countless studies showing the impact to the bottom line.

In early 2007, during the heyday of my LGBTQ marketing outreach and my ability to pursue what I felt was in the best interest of my employer, I stumbled into a whole new world. Something out of Alice in Wonderland—okay, maybe not that dramatic—but at the time it felt that way.

Having been given carte blanche to craft the campaign, I spent quite a bit of time researching and vetting opportunities I felt were going to get me to my $1 million revenue goal. It was during this time that I discovered Community Marketing Inc., Harris Interactive and The Williams Institute at UCLA. While

I learned of these companies over a decade ago, they are still relevant today. Please spend some time looking at their websites. They offer volumes of information that will help you articulate why the LGBTQ market is important.

The other organization I encountered during this time was a game changer. It literally changed my life's trajectory. One day I stumbled upon the National Gay & Lesbian Chamber of Commerce (NGLCC). I wasn't 100% certain what a chamber of commerce was or how this organization could help my employer, but without much information I promptly signed up to become a member.

At the time, being a member of the National Gay & Lesbian Chamber of Commerce did not immediately yield business opportunities. They held an annual conference and published a membership directory, but that was the extent of it.

You may recall from the previous chapter that my relationship with my employer ended when I hit the breaking point—the point at which I couldn't reconcile what I was saying publicly versus what was happening to me internally. This is where my story diverges. This is how I found what I was truly meant to be doing in life.

> I hit the breaking point—the point at which I couldn't reconcile what I was saying publicly versus what was happening to me internally. This is where my story diverges. This is how I found what I was truly meant to be doing in life.

In the Summer of 2007 I received a phone call from a woman who was starting a Connecticut affiliate (i.e. a chapter) of NGLCC.

She had been searching NGLCC's national database

to find local contacts to engage with in this newly forming organization. She found my name, employer, and title listed in the directory. Having been listed as the Marketing Coordinator, she asked if we could meet to discuss my helping her with this new organization.

Shortly after that first conversation, she called me at home one evening. When she offered me the volunteer role of 'Marketing Committee Chair' I immediately said YES!

For several months I worked with the founder and other founding board members to create our marketing campaign and to prepare for the launch of our local affiliate.

We officially launched in October 2007 at a restaurant in New Haven. Over 100 business owners and professionals came out to see what we were all about. At age 26, this was my first local business after hours style networking event.

It was at this event that I found the secret to navigating networking events—work the registration table! Crazy, right? At the time I was very shy. I struggled with speaking in front of a crowd or with more than a couple of people at once, so working the registration table was amazing! I was able to say hello to every single person who attended the event, in a one-on-one interaction. I got to see their names, their business or who they worked for. Then it was simple enough to go find them later and start a conversation.

If you are nervous about attending an LGBTQ event, contact the organizer and ask how you can volunteer. When you have a specific role it can ease the transition into a new environment.

Thinking back on it now, I wish there was a way to bottle the energy and spirit of a grassroots LGBTQ organization. It provided me with hope and with a sense that there was a place for me in this world. My fellow board members and our broader membership became part of my family. When I hit rough patches in my personal life throughout this time, they all had my back and vice versa. I learned so much from my peers about business, about the LGBTQ community, and about coming out in the workplace. It was incredibly powerful.

This is how I was able to find *my* community. Let's talk about how you find yours. How do you find where you belong in this seemingly complex LGBTQ landscape?

There are a couple of very easy ways.

Back when I was 26 I didn't know what a chamber of commerce was or what one did, so following in my footsteps isn't advised. Yet somehow I found *my* place in this world.

What you can do as your first step is to look around your local LGBTQ community and identify organizations that align with your interests. This could be around business interests or personal interests. If you are doing something you are interested in and passionate about it will show in everything that you do.

For example, you may be a proponent of healthcare rights and issues within your state. You might also have a business that dovetails with this interest. For you, finding the local LGBTQ health collective organization would be a natural place to get involved.

Similarly, you may love theatre and singing. You may want to consider getting involved in the local LGBTQ choir group. You will, of course, have to do your homework with any organization you are considering becoming involved in.

Your next step, after having identified organizations of interest, is to contact their executive director, if they have one. If they don't have an executive director, reach out to the president of the board of directors, or any other board member you may have a connection to.

Explain to the organization that you are an ally looking to get involved in the LGBTQ community. Ask them how you could help their organization and share your thoughts on how you could contribute. At this point you should also mention any hesitations or concerns you might be feeling as an ally newly approaching this. I have found that more often than not you will be met with a warm response.

Once you have the green light, get yourself out there and start being the best damn ally you can be!

CHAPTER 3

HOW I DISCOVERED MY 'WHY'

A S 2009 CAME to a close and our chamber was riding the high of having won the Rising Star Chamber award, we knew, as a Board comprised of volunteers, that we had to make a change by hiring someone who could take us higher. Without really even thinking about it I threw my hat into the ring based on two facts: (1) by this point I absolutely hated my day job and; (2) I was head over heels in love with this world of LGBTQ business ownership, both locally and nationally.

As part of my volunteer work, I was invited to be part of the national conversation. I proudly held a volunteer leadership position with NGLCC. I had the honor to be appointed as Chair of the Mid-Atlantic and Northeast Regions for the Council of Chambers and Business Organizations. This leveled up my vantage point on the state of LGBTQ business in our country. As a council we convened to discuss best practices for our local chamber members. We would share ideas, success stories and sometimes war stories of what was going on in our local communities.

I had found my calling, helping people grow their businesses.

> I had found my calling, helping people grow their businesses.

When I skipped right on out of my day job at the insurance company, I also said goodbye to benefits and a steady paycheck and said hello to my first contractor position. On December 1, 2009 I became the first Executive Director of the Connecticut LGBTQ Chamber of Commerce.

When I started the position, I wasn't exactly sure what an Executive Director did, but it didn't matter, I was on a mission to take this organization to the next level. I went from being a total wallflower at the first event—to being shoved in front of the room—to running the organization a short two years later. There's no better way to master public speaking than by being thrown into it!

My primary job as the Executive Director was to help our members grow their businesses, connect with one another, and help drive economic opportunities within the State of Connecticut. Every single day I was asked questions like—"How do I market to this community?", "How do I market to gay men?", and "How do I market to lesbians?" These questions were asked by the smallest small business, the high-growth stable business and executives at Fortune 500 companies. They were asking the same questions, and they expected me to have all the answers.

During my tenure as Executive Director, which lasted almost four years, I worked with hundreds of business owners, corporations, and non-profits both locally and nationally. I made it a point to learn as much as I could about each of these businesses in order to help them market their goods and services to the LGBTQ community in the way that would yield the best results.

When members asked these types of questions, I would sit down with them, preferably at their business, and I would ask *a lot* of questions. I couldn't just give a stock answer, I needed to know the business, understand their business model, get a handle on who their customers were, and then, only then, could I give them a specific answer that would point them in the right direction of doing it properly.

I watched many of my members nail this. They were amazing and their businesses were rocking and rolling while working with the LGBTQ community. I also watched members fail miserably. Their lack of understanding as to why they were doing it or not properly communicating their intentions, proved to be a tricky situation.

> Every single day I was asked questions like—"How do I market to this community?", "How do I market to gay men?", and "How do I market to lesbians?" These questions were asked by the smallest small business, the high-growth stable business and executives at Fortune 500 companies. They were asking the same questions, and they expected me to have all the answers.

The nuance of any market can be tricky, but the LGBTQ community has its own set of nuances that can be fraught, if not approached properly.

In September 2012 I had an epiphany. One day I had been talking to two business people on the phone and thought, if only someone could be a fly on the wall—the amount that they would learn from this conversation would be incredible. Then it hit me, I should start a podcast! I spent the Fall learning how to podcast and launched it in January 2013.

Around this same time I was texting with one of my best friends. She was asking me how to work with one of her transgender patients. Specifically, she was asking how to broach the topic of their sexual history without making them uncomfortable. This was not the first time she had asked a question like this. In fact, she continues to ask LGBTQ specific questions to this day!

I had a second epiphany during that conversation—if these types of questions were coming up regularly for her, how many other nurse practitioners or medical professionals were wondering the same things? In November 2012 I started my blog by answering her very first question.

The blog became my faithful companion. I would write twice a week on communication and/or marketing related topics—and every single post stemmed from a recent experience I had. Oftentimes, it was a recent interaction with a local Connecticut chamber member, other times it was something in my personal life. With each blog written and podcast recorded I had one goal in mind—to educate the reader or listener on how to effectively connect with the LGBTQ community. This was a wonderful and cathartic experience. I've always loved writing and there were so many things I was learning from my members locally, and from my peers nationally, that was applicable across state borders. I never ran out of something to talk about.

In March 2013, after a strong run as the chamber's first Executive Director I put in my resignation. This was such a hard decision. I truly loved my board members, volunteers, members and the impact we were making on Connecticut's economy. But my national experience, and the excitement of my new blog and podcast, pulled me into another direction—a direction where I could impact a larger number of people.

I set out on this endeavor with just a hunch—I suspected that my local experience to date working with the LGBTQ community and business owners, corporations, non-profits, etc. would be applicable outside of Connecticut. I believed that my years of working locally would translate and resonate with people in Texas or Michigan. I'm pleased to say my prediction was accurate.

Shortly after starting my blog and podcast I began hearing from people all over the world. I was receiving emails from people in countries I hadn't previously heard of. They were seeking advice, wanting me to answer their specific questions, and generally trying to do good for their local LGBTQ community. The nuance from state to state, country to country, or geographic subsets in a state or country are vast, but I attempted to tackle them in the most honest way possible.

At some point during my tenure as the chamber's Executive Director, I began jokingly calling myself a professional lesbian. This started off as a joke but it began to stick. It would do two things; (1) stop people in their tracks who wanted to know more about what a 'professional lesbian' did and; (2) it would break the ice or ease the tension in a situation where I may have been meeting with someone who was just setting out on their path to learning about the LGBTQ community.

Humor has a way of loosening people up and the more I began using the moniker the more it began to catch on. As I began pivoting my marketing to focus on myself as a personal brand, the speaking opportunities and consulting contracts began flowing.

To be an entrepreneur, there is some level of A.D.D. or bright, shiny object syndrome happening. We rapidly move from one thing to the next. Working with Fortune 500 clients and small soloprenuers fed that need for variety in my life, and also equipped me with a well-rounded view of the social and economic landscape of the LGBTQ community.

Today I have the incredible privilege of traveling around the world as the Professional Lesbian. I speak, empower and motivate business owners and corporate professionals alike, as well as conduct trainings and consulting. The ability to impact, and advocate for, LGBTQ people in all facets of their professional lives is what being the Professional Lesbian is all about.

CHAPTER 4

WHAT'S YOUR ROLE?

A S YOU CONTINUE to read this book, terminology is going to pop up that you may or may not be familiar with. In addition to having a glossary in the back of this book, I'll be introducing terms, concepts and new approaches that are woven throughout each story.

Here are the first three terms that relate to the LGBTQ community—ally, advocate and activist. I suspect you could be considered one already—just by the fact that you are reading this book.

Side note: It's important that we don't get bogged down with labels here. The following terms are applicable in any context of your life, but we want to remain focused on your role as a business owner or corporate professional.

An Ally is "a heterosexual person who supports equal civil rights, gender equality, and LGBTQ social movements, and who challenges homophobia and transphobia. A straight ally believes that LGBTQ people face discrimination and thus are socially and economically disadvantaged. Straight allies aim to use their position as heterosexual and/or cisgender individuals in a society focused on heteronormativity to fight homophobia and transphobia."[3] (Later we will define any new words from this definition.)

An Advocate is "a person who speaks or writes in support or defense of a person, cause, etc. or a person who pleads for or on behalf of another; intercessor."[4]

Activism and activists, "in a general sense, can be described as intentional action to bring about social change, political change, economic justice, or environmental well-being. This action is in support of, or opposition to, one side of an often controversial argument.

The word Activism "is often used synonymously with protest or dissent, but activism can stem from any number of political orientations and take a wide range of forms, from writing letters to newspapers or politicians, political campaigning, economic activism (such as boycotts or preferentially patronizing preferred businesses), rallies, blogging and street marches, strikes, both work stoppages and hunger strikes, or even guerrilla tactics."[5]

Which one are you?

Who are you? An ally? An activist? Or an advocate?

Trick question. You don't have to choose. The important thing is that you understand the differences between these words, their meanings and recognize a compliment when you are paid one!

---

3 http://en.wikipedia.org/wiki/Straight_ally

4 http://www.dictionary.com/browse/advocate

5 https://en.wikipedia.org/wiki/Activism

I've come to realize how murky these words are for people. In one conversation I said, "It's great to have an ally like you." The person reacted very dismissively. Upon asking why he reacted like that, I discovered it was because he thought I was referring to him as a political activist/advocate. Once I explained the true meaning to him, he was honored I would consider him such.

I had a similar conversation while Tweeting with an incredibly high-powered banker. When I said, "It's great to have allies like you helping to support the LGBTQ cause," he was confused and insulted by the word ally until I explained what it meant. Then he was honored.

To me, an ally is a person who is supportive of the LGBTQ community. An ally is someone who has friends, family or colleagues who are part of the LGBTQ community and has a vested interest in supporting the community in their business or their workplace.

It is important to note that we *all* have the ability to be an ally. For example, as a lesbian, I am an ally to the transgender community. I am not transgender but I support equal rights and protections for the T in the LGBTQ community.

I believe if each person reading this book can definitively say, with confidence and compassion, "I am an ally" to the LGBTQ community or a subset within the community, we are already on an incredibly unified path.

Change Happens in Business

Let me be 100% clear—if you are looking to do business with the LGBTQ community, you *must* be proactive and take action to benefit the LGBTQ community. One of my mantras is

Change Happens in Business. It does. Businesses, corporate environments and small family owned businesses don't just decide they are going to make change on behalf of a marginalized community—the people in the business make the decision.

And you, yes you, are the person I am referring to.

You must take it a step further than merely attending an LGBTQ networking event or putting an ad in a program book. Doing those things is a good starting point, but there are significant ways in which you can be an incredible change maker for the LGBTQ community.

Let me give you an example.

Same-sex marriage was passed in the State of Connecticut in the Fall of 2008. Prior to the court ruling I took direction from those around me on how to advocate for our right to marry. Advocacy comes in many different forms and fashions. For example, you can contact your local elected officials by phone, email, written letter or rally a group of like-minded individuals to make your voice heard.

An incredible organization, Love Makes A Family, led the charge for marriage equality in Connecticut. They shouldered the grassroots efforts and rallied the community. Our job as the local LGBTQ chamber was to facilitate the discussion on marriage equality as a significant economic driver in the state. As an individual, I called my legislators and I lobbied at the state capitol. I made my individual voice heard.

Here is where you have the power:

Entrepreneurs, soloprenuers, business owners and corporations have a voice bigger than anyone elses. Small business owners make the economy go round. They have incredible influence on the local level because they employ people, pay taxes, and put money directly back into the local economy. Corporations have the ability to set themselves apart by changing internal policies that impact the LGBTQ community, and by providing safe job opportunities.

During the overturning of the Defense of Marriage Act (DOMA) in 2013, the law firm Bingham McCutchen sought out employers to sign an Amicus Brief in the legal case Windsor v. United States. The intent of this was to illustrate the amount of businesses that supported marriage equality—to make the economic case for overturning DOMA.

> If you are looking to do business with the LGBTQ community, you *must* be proactive and take action to benefit the LGBTQ community.

While I am incredibly proud to have been one of the businesses that signed the Amicus Brief, the fact of the matter is only 278 employers signed on. The point was made and DOMA was overturned in 2013. However, *only* 278 employers signed this Amicus Brief out of the millions of businesses and corporations in America.

Often, the reason businesses aren't signing on to items like this is because they don't see the opportunity. As a business owner you can stand unified with the best businesses for LGBTQ equality. You will become known as a supporter of full inclusion of LGBTQ people in business. This is a huge factor when an LGBTQ consumer is deciding between your business and your competitors. Who stood up for equality when they weren't forced to? Who was proactive? That's who will win the business.

What I want you to do from here is to pay attention, listen to the conversation—hell—insert yourself into the conversation.

The conversation is happening, so find ways that you can lend your valuable economic business voice to it.

How? Start with the national level of an organization. Find out what they are about, who they serve and who they are advocating for. Ask them what you can do on a local level and chances are they will connect you with their local representatives.

There are many different kinds of LGBTQ and allied organizations advocating on behalf of the community. To make this task easier for you, I've compiled a list of the top organizations in the references section in the back of this book.

The minimal amount of effort this takes is worth every second. I promise you this.

> The conversation is happening, so find ways that you can lend your valuable economic business voice to it.

I am proud to have been one of the 278 businesses that signed on to the Amicus Brief. The attorneys at Bingham McCutchen sent me a signed copy of the Amicus Brief, a treasured piece of my American history (photo).

CHAPTER 5

·· ·

UNCOVERING YOUR 'WHY'

HAVING ENGAGED IN thousands of conversations around LGBTQ topics, primarily through a business lens, I've gotten into a very good groove of uncovering someone's motives—fast. Naturally, you are looking to do business with the LGBTQ community because you see the economic opportunities, so yes, of course—impacting your business is a top goal. But the real opportunity is that you can change lives, even save lives, by using your ally voice to support your LGBTQ customers, colleagues and employees.

Here's how I uncover someone's motives.

I ask them one, very simple, question.

Why?

That's it. Why?

Why are *you* looking to do business with the LGBTQ community? Why is this important to you? What personal experience do you have with the community that has impacted your decision to do this?

I cannot steer an insincere person toward the LGBTQ community and sleep at night knowing I've done such a thing. If I'm going to consult with an organization it is because I believe in them, they believe in the community, and as a result we can make change happen in business, together.

I don't want you to be worried or concerned about how to answer this question.

However, it is important to reflect for a moment and think about what your gut response is. You don't have to tell me—or anyone else— just sit with your answer for a moment. Your first response is likely your best response.

> I cannot steer an insincere person toward the LGBTQ community and sleep at night knowing I've done such a thing. If I'm going to consult with an organization it is because I believe in them, they believe in the community, and as a result we can make change happen in business, together.

I've heard responses that range from "My daughter is gay and I want to support her in my business" to "I have a lot of LGBTQ employees and I want to make their workplace safe and comfortable." As you recall, the latter response would have been heavenly in the toxic work environment I survived in for five years!

I have a challenge for you. I want you to come up with five reasons why you want to engage the LGBTQ community. I don't want you to spend an hour thinking about this, I simply want you to brain dump your top five reasons. Grab a pen and let's do it! Write your answers (or don't, if you don't like writing in books, like I don't).

Don't overthink this, just write.

1. _____

_____

2. _____

_____

3. _____

_____

4. _____

_____

5. _____

_____

TIME'S UP!

Were you able to come up with five reasons? What about three reasons? One?

Through my work, I've heard hundreds of reasons of why organizations and entrepreneurs decide to invest in an LGBTQ outreach effort. But there is one story that has stayed with me for many years.

Terry's 'Why'

A few years back, I was introduced to Terry through a mutual friend. Terry owns a company that focuses on fashion. As a stylist, she helps women find the right clothing in order to boost their confidence and their careers.

Not knowing much about Terry or her business, I was delighted to talk with her over a cup of coffee. My first question to her was my big one: Why? I wanted to know why she had chosen to become an active part of the LGBTQ Chamber of Commerce. I was delighted by her unfiltered response.

Many years ago, Terry worked for a women's clothier. One morning, Terry received a call from a woman inquiring about the privacy of the fitting rooms. She asked if there was a quieter time of day when she could come in and try on clothing. Terry's initial response was standard, "You can come down any time you'd like."

The woman on the line went silent, then nervously said, "I just need you to know that I am transitioning. I was born a man and am transitioning to a woman, but I've not fully done so yet." The woman was concerned that her not fully female appearance might make some other shoppers uncomfortable.

This experience took place in 1987, so before reading on, let me ask you this, "What do you think your reaction would have been?" This situation happened 30 years ago, when marriage equality wasn't even a talking point, and states did not have any workplace protections against LGBTQ discrimination. I ask you this because the true intent of an ally can be put to the test in a spontaneous moment like this.

Terry handled the situation with grace and care, "I would

love to work with you. I do have to be respectful of my other customers and I thank you for being sensitive to that. We are the slowest on Wednesday mornings so let's set up an appointment. You'll have more privacy and I can spend more time helping you select the right clothing for your body type."

On a surface level you could view this conversation as a simple act of customer service. But it was more than that. The woman calling Terry's store was looking for a safe place to try on clothing. We don't know how many other places she called before finding Terry. To this day I wonder how other stores treated her.

Terry's allyship[6] went further. She put a safety plan in place with this customer to ensure she, and the other customers, were able to all use the fitting room while maintaining comfort and respect for all involved. Terry recalled that she enjoyed a chat with the woman after the experience where she was able to open up more—and where Terry ultimately felt she was able to connect with another human well beyond their clothing needs.

I'm confident Terry's acceptance had a profound impact on this woman's life. Coming out as LGBQ can be incredibly difficult and painful, with limited family support and the loss of many friendships. This is magnified when someone comes out as transgender. The woman she assisted that day was probably going through a difficult patch in her life and Terry was likely that rainbow that gave the woman much needed hope.

This is why Terry joined the LGBTQ Chamber of Commerce. She knew there would be women within the chamber who needed

---

6 https://theantioppressionnetwork.wordpress.com/allyship/

her services. She wanted to provide that safe space for women to find their new style without fear of humiliation and discrimination.

The real Terry

It can be challenging when asked to make referrals to people within the LGBTQ community. But when you come across someone like Terry, it's easy to refer her to an LGBTQ person. In the grand scheme, someone being part of the LGBTQ community *should not* matter in a business setting. The person with the best product or service should be what matters. But guess what? We are not there yet. Being LGBTQ is a huge factor in determining who is safe to do business with. People's safety and dignity are on the line. Referring Terry and allies like Terry is a no-brainer.

I want you to understand that there is a spectrum of '*whys*'—and yours will likely fall somewhere on the spectrum. I want you to think about your *why*, work with it, and examine it.

CHAPTER 6

THE WRONG KIND OF 'WHY'

O UT OF THE hundreds of '*whys*' I've heard through the years, Terry's falls on the far left of the spectrum. I want you to be like Terry. But on the far right of the spectrum falls Richard and Bob. I do *not* want you to be like them, and here's why.

In my work as the Professional Lesbian, I liaise with marketing and advertising agencies on a regular basis. These agencies often find themselves tasked with creating a campaign that will reach the LGBTQ community. The agency will recognize they don't have that expertise in-house and will reach out to me for behind-the-scenes support. I love being part of LGBTQ strategy work!

Years ago a local advertising agency reached out to me for this exact reason. A potential client of theirs, a financial firm, wanted to reach the LGBTQ market. In preparation for this meeting the client provided us with a summary, which outlined their '*why?*' With limited knowledge of this firm, or the owners of it, I arrived to the discovery meeting with a dozen ideas of how they could strategically reach the community.

We sat down in the conference room with two gentlemen, Richard and Bob, and immediately got down to brass tacks.

When I learned this firm was associated with a major financial institution, I immediately saw a red flag. But I decided to dismiss it, at least for the moment, so I could learn more about the client and their objectives.

The first red flag was their score on the Human Rights Campaign's (HRC) Corporate Equality Index (CEI). The CEI rates companies on a scale of -25 to 100 based on their policies and practices relating to the LGBTQ community. They held a 10 (out of 100). This score served as a warning sign that there was a significant misalignment between the financial institution and the LGBTQ community. In this case, the corporation had been evaluated by the HRC. However, we were meeting a local office.

I've worked with many firms and independent agents across the country, who very much supported and were proactive within the LGBTQ community, even if corporate was not.

> Remember, LGBTQ customers are looking for safe places to do business where they don't have to worry that their identity is going to be a factor in the level of service they are provided.

I began to explain that corporate's low CEI score would make our efforts that much more challenging. When your competition has a 100 in relation to your 10, that difference is significant. Remember, LGBTQ customers are looking for safe places to do business where they don't have to worry that their identity is going to be a factor in the level of service they are provided. But when I asked them for their 'why' document, the word homosexual caught my eye and my heart sank.

Their number one 'why' was outlined as follows, *research shows gays have a higher disposable income with less children.*

You already know that seeing the LGBTQ community as a viable market opportunity is a perfectly acceptable business strategy. But now you also know that this strategy must be equally backed up by motives that are sincere and authentic.

> You already know that seeing the LGBTQ community as a viable market opportunity is a perfectly acceptable business strategy. But now you also know that this strategy must be equally backed up by motives that are sincere and authentic.

These client saw the LGBTQ community with dollar signs in their eyes. They wanted to throw large sums of advertising dollars at their local market and they fully expected a high return on their investment—simply because they had seen statistics that showed 'gays' have a higher disposable income.

Sidebar: I advise not using the term 'gays' as a general descriptor for the community in any setting. It comes across disrespectful, ignorant and dated—even *if* that is not your intention. Most often people who are anti-gay, or anti-LGBTQ, will prove their points by saying something derogatory about the community, such as "Gays are an abomination." This is an avoidable situation and not something you want to get caught in. Using the preferred language in interactions with the LGBTQ community is critical. You'll learn more of what that preferred language is as we go.

During our 90-minute meeting I had tried repeatedly to uncover their why. I've heard so many that I know if I ask the right follow up questions I can find something good to work with. But in this meeting we were going nowhere—fast.

It didn't take long before I could see that whether it was their written, verbal or non-verbal communications, their blatant lack of understanding and immediate dismissal of my recommendations, was going to be a major problem. For example, they would not budge on their flagrant and incessant use of the word homosexual. Even after explaining to them why they should use LGBT or LGBTQ versus homosexual, they kept on using it.

Over the years, I've had more encounters than I can count where people had *no* idea that the word homosexual was something that they should not use. This may be one of the top misconceptions when it comes to the LGBTQ community. In 95% of those encounters it was pure lack of understanding. No ill will intended, just simply not understanding that this is a phrase that the LGBTQ community would prefer you avoid. Once I bring this information to light, the person typically says something about not having known and they won't intentionally do it again. With these gentlemen, that was not the case.

Sidebar: Let's talk about why you shouldn't use the word homosexual, then we'll get back to the story.

If you Google the word homosexual, three common themes pop up—clinical associations, the Bible, and marriage. All three of these things are not something you want to be associated with. Here are three reasons you should stop saying homosexual immediately.

1. The word homosexual has a clinical history to it. Considered a mental disorder until 1973, many anti-gay/anti-LGBTQ people use homosexual as a politically charged derogatory slang term.

2. The second theme is associated with the Bible. There is a passage in Corinthians that uses the word homosexual. This is the passage that every anti-gay/anti-LGBTQ individual grabs a hold of to make his or her case against LGBTQ rights.

3. Finally, the same-sex marriage debate. If you listen to anyone who is opposed to LGBTQ people getting married, you will inevitably hear them say "Homosexual marriage is harmful," "Homosexuals getting married is a sin," and "Homosexuality will ruin the sanctity of marriage." Homosexual is the calculated choice word of the anti-gay/anti-LGBTQ movement. Clearly, this is not how you would want to position yourself in the market, right?

Here's an innocent example of what this might look like in a conversation. I was meeting with a straight friend/colleague and she said to me, while referring to a mutual person we knew, "Well he may not be an asshole to you because I think he's a closeted homosexual."

I gently called her out on what she said, and after a quick discussion of what she said and how it sounded to me, she was immediately embarrassed. Her intended point in saying this to me really had nothing to do with the word homosexual, her point was that she didn't think this particular person was a jackass to me because he was gay, just not out of the closet. Had her phrase been "Well he may not be an asshole to you because I think he's in the closet," that has an *entirely* different meaning.

She genuinely had no idea calling someone homosexual instead of gay or LGBTQ was a bad thing. She simply didn't know that the word homosexual is riddled with negative connotations. I'm willing to bet there is a 50/50 chance that you didn't either. Guess what? That's okay. This is why you are reading this book, so you can learn and take action. This benefits you a great deal, but equally benefits the community.

Back to Richard & Bob

Now that you are familiar with why you shouldn't say homosexual, let's get back to the financial firm and their incessant usage of the word. Despite my repeated efforts to explain to them why they shouldn't say homosexual, it fell on deaf ears. They truly had no desire to change their language or their perception of the LGBTQ community.

They were so wrapped up in how they were going to make money. The whole meeting felt sleazy and disingenuous. I could not get a *why* out of them that was not wrapped purely in greed.

I knew midway through this meeting that I had no desire to help this financial firm reach the LGBTQ market. After the meeting concluded I politely told the agency that I was not willing to put my name on the line to help this firm who clearly did not care about the LGBTQ community. The clients had a lot of money to throw at this campaign, which could have made me money that day, but my responsibility above all else is to protect the LGBTQ community from companies and individuals like these men—those who are out to make a quick buck at the expense of exploiting the community.

That is my '*why*.'

This was not the first time I've turned down business like this, and certainly won't be the last. I didn't follow the advertising agency so I have no idea what their clients decided to do next. But I did see one of the owners of that financial firm at an LGBTQ event years later. Based on how people were interacting with him in the room, it was clear he wasn't doing well, which

> The clients had a lot of money to throw at this campaign, which could have made me money that day, but my responsibility above all else is to protect the LGBTQ community from companies and individuals like these men—those who are out to make a quick buck at the expense of exploiting the community.

I could have predicted. There was a stench to his inauthenticity that LGBTQ people could immediately pick up on. Don't be like Richard or Bob.

CHAPTER 7

THE HIDDEN NUANCE OF LGBTQ TERMINOLOGY

REGARDLESS OF WHAT community of people you are trying to reach within your business, whether they are LGBTQ or otherwise, you have 60 seconds to make a good impression. It can also take less than 60 seconds to ruin that previously created good impression.

If you are actively engaging the LGBTQ community by attending events, building relationships and marketing to attract new LGBTQ customers or employees, you are sending a clear message, and setting an expectation. The unstated expectation is that you and your company are open for business within the LGBTQ community. So what happens when someone from the community is treated differently, like an outsider, or is somehow on the receiving end of a disparaging comment? Disaster can strike.

Acronym Alphabet Soup

I intentionally waited until this point of the book to get into the nuts and bolts of terminology. I need you to be in the proper headspace to fully wrap your head around some of what we will cover.

Whether you are beginning this journey or have been at it for years, you'll hear a variety of acronyms that include; LGBT, GLBT, LGBTQ, or LGBTQIA, among others.

They stand for the following* -

- LGBT: Lesbian, Gay, Bisexual, Transgender

- GLBT: Gay, Lesbian, Bisexual, Transgender

- LGBTQ: Lesbian, Gay, Bisexual, Transgender, Queer (or Questioning); This is the acronym of choice when refer-ring to the entire community in a general way.

- LGBTQIA: Lesbian, Gay, Bisexual, Transgender, Queer/ Questioning, Intersex, Asexual (or Ally)

We will define all of these shortly!

You may feel overwhelmed by the litany of options. I advise you use LGBT or LGBTQ and here's why.

The LGBTQ community is constantly evolving. Here's a timeline which outlines how my own language has changed over the past decade.

When I began working in the community over 10 years ago, the preferred acronym was GLBT. Using GLBT today isn't wrong per se, however, it does raise eyebrows among members of the community because it sounds antiquated, and sends a signal that you are not current.

I've consistently used and advised people to use LGBT since I transitioned away from GLBT in 2007. In 2015, I began migrating toward LGBTQ away from LGBT. The Q has been added and used more frequently to provide an identity for the broader LGBT community. In many ways, lesbian, gay, bisexual and transgender can be very limiting from an identity standpoint. Adding Q for queer (or sometimes questioning) broadens the possibilities to include all people who do not fit traditional gender norms.

Over the last few years I've seen LGBTQ organizations adopt and embrace the Q, with it meaning queer. However, I have not seen a significant level of adoption by organizations outside the community—yet. As an ally reader you are probably safer to use LGBT because it is a tried and true term with limited amounts of offense that can be inflicted. But if you want to come out of the gate strong, bold and inclusive, LGBTQ can certainly help you do that.

Let's break down this acronym further:

"Gay is a term that primarily refers to a homosexual person or the trait of being homosexual. In modern English, 'gay' has come to be used as an adjective and as a noun, referring to the people, especially to males, and the practices and cultures associated with homosexuality."[7]

"Lesbian is the term most widely used in the English language to describe sexual and romantic attraction between females. The word may be used as a noun to refer to women who identify

7 http://en.wikipedia.org/wiki/Gay

themselves or who are characterized by others as having the primary attribute of female homosexuality, or as an adjective to describe characteristics of an object or activity related to female same-sex attraction."[8]

"Bisexuality is romantic attraction, sexual attraction or sexual behavior toward both males and females. The term is mainly used in the context of human attraction to denote romantic or sexual feelings toward both men and women. It may also be defined as encompassing romantic or sexual attraction to people of all gender identities or to a person irrespective of that person's biological sex or gender, which is sometimes termed pansexuality."[9]

But these definitions may be much lesser known.

"Pansexuality, or omnisexuality, is sexual attraction, sexual desire, romantic love, or emotional attraction toward people of all gender identities and biological sexes. Self-identified pansexuals may consider pansexuality a sexual orientation, and refer to themselves as gender-blind, asserting that gender and sex are insignificant or irrelevant in determining whether they will be sexually attracted to others."[10]

"Asexuality (or nonsexuality) is the lack of sexual attraction to anyone or low or absent interest in sexual activity. It may be considered the lack of a sexual orientation, or one of the four types thereof, alongside heterosexuality, homosexuality, and bisexuality. A study in 2004 placed the prevalence of asexuality at 1%."[11]

---

8 http://en.wikipedia.org/wiki/Lesbian

9 http://en.wikipedia.org/wiki/Bisexual

10 http://en.wikipedia.org/wiki/Pansexuality

11 http://en.wikipedia.org/wiki/Asexuality

"Intersex is a variation in sex characteristics including chromosomes, gonads, and/or genitals that do not allow an individual to be distinctly identified as male or female. Intersex infants with ambiguous outer genitalia may be surgically 'corrected' to more easily fit into a socially accepted sex category. Others may opt, in adulthood, for surgical procedures in order to align their physical sex characteristics with their gender identity or the sex category to which they were assigned at birth. Some individuals may be raised as a certain sex (male or female) but then identify with another later in life, while others may not identify themselves as either exclusively female or exclusively male."[12]

Are you still with me? Let's go a layer deeper.

A term that often pops up when discussing the transgender community, is the word cisgender. I can tell you for a fact that there are a lot of people within the LGBTQ community itself who do not know what the word cisgender means. Yes, even the community can be confused sometimes—you are not alone.

"Cisgender and cissexual (often abbreviated to simply cis) describe related types of gender identity where an individual's self-perception of their gender matches the sex they were assigned at birth."[13]

Cisgender is a term that is used to describe a person who identifies as the gender they were assigned at birth. So you may be asking yourself, why do we need such a term? Well, it's because cisgender is a way to describe someone who is not transgender. It's a more correct way of saying non-transgender. Saying

---

12 http://en.wikipedia.org/wiki/Intersex

13 http://en.wikipedia.org/wiki/Cisgender

non-transgender makes an implication that being transgender is abnormal, whereas saying cisgender and transgender doesn't make any implications in either direction. They are simply two words with equal meanings coexisting together.

This is a very simplistic definition of what cisgender is. It is important to note that while the terms transgender and cisgender are used together, sex and gender are not the same thing, nor are gender identity and sexual orientation, which we will get into shortly.

Now, I want to spend a good amount of time discussing the TQ in LGBTQ. For the most part the terms listed above are straightforward, however, once we get into transgender and queer, we start to see many of the hidden meanings and context of each of these words, and how this can inadvertently offend someone within the community. I want the LGBTQ community to feel comfortable working with you and I want you to feel comfortable working within it.

Transgender

The transgender community is often misunderstood and overlooked—even by people within the LGBTQ itself. This drives me crazy!

To better serve this often-underrepresented community, let's discuss some important terms.

- Transgender: Refers to a person whose gender identity, one's deeply internalized sense of self as a man or a woman, is different than the gender identity typically associated with the person's sex at birth.[14]

- Transgender man: A term for a transgender individual who identifies as a man.

- Transgender woman: A term for a transgender individual who identifies as a woman.

- Gender identity: An individual's internal sense of being male or female. Since gender identity is internal, one's gender identity is not necessarily visible to others.

- Gender expression: How a person represents or expresses one's gender identity to others, often through behavior, clothing, hairstyles, voice, or body characteristics.

- Gender non-conforming: A term for individuals whose gender expression is different from societal expectations related to gender.

I will get into more detail on what each of those bullet points means shortly. But I'd like to explain to you some of the problematic terms that come up as they relate to the transgender community. I share these with you so you do not inadvertently say something offensive.

---

14 https://www.merriam-webster.com/dictionary/transgender

Curiosity Killed the Cat

"Transgendered" is a word that is often used incorrectly. When broken down, it is trans + gender. The prefix meaning of *trans* is 'to cross' or 'to go beyond.' In its root form, transgender means 'to cross genders.'

So when the *-ed* gets added to the end to create 'transgendered,' it's essentially the equivalent of saying lesbianed. I wouldn't walk up to someone and say, "Hi, my name is Jenn and I'm lesbianed." Just as you wouldn't hear someone say, "Hey, my name is Tony and I'm transgendered."

It is important to bring this up because I hear it happen *all the time*. The fact is that when someone says transgendered it by no means implies that the person saying it isn't inclusive or that they are intentionally trying to be offensive. However, someone may hear you say transgendered and make an assumption that you are a fake or a phony trying to solicit business from the LGBTQ community without being sincere and genuine. This is clearly the last thing you want to have happen, especially over a simple mistake that can be avoided. Those two simple letters 'ed' added to the end of a word can convey a message that is diametrically opposed to your intent. I know this is not your intent, and you know this is not your intent, but the community may not know it, so let's avoid it altogether.

There is more nuance around the transgender community than I can fit in this book, but I do want to spend some time covering the bigger issues I see on a regular basis.

A question that I've been asked many times after presenting at conferences or even in client meetings is, "Can I ask a transgender person what their 'other name' was?" The answer to this is *always* no. This is not an appropriate question to ask. Ever. Period.

I want you to think for a moment and ask yourself a few questions that you can apply to any setting, really—

1. Does obtaining this bit of information have any bearing on your relationship with the person you are speaking with?

2. Does having this information allow you to better serve them as a client/customer, or work with them as a colleague?

3. Would you be upset if someone asked you something similar to this?

If the information has no relevance to your customer, colleague or employee, don't ask it. I don't care how curious you are, just don't do it. No good outcome will come from this. When we are referring specifically to asking this question of someone from the transgender community, you have to put yourself in their shoes and understand what you are asking and what that is implying.

I have a very dear friend who is a transgender man and he mistakenly told someone his name given at birth, which was a female name. He told me that on numerous occasions this person would accidentally use his previous female name, even though this person had never known him other than who he was, as a man. This is a very problematic situation because it makes people uncomfortable, not just the transgender person whom you are clearly offending, but also anyone around to bear witness to this awkward situation.

This same friend and I were hosting an event together, which included a live Q&A at the end. Having a live Q&A can be risky for any kind of event, but the risk factor increases when the topic is LGBTQ, more specifically transgender. The uncertainty of what someone might ask, the possibility of being caught off guard by a question or being heckled or berated from a crowd are all chances you take.

At this particular event, the question, "What was your other name?" was asked. Fortunately, I work beside some amazing people who are highly skilled when working with a crowd. My friend who was fielding this inquiry responded with a question of his own, "Why does my given name at birth matter?" The audience member sputtered out that she was curious.

As a general rule of thumb, nine out of 10 times, there is no good reason to ask what you might be thinking. If you are debating whether it is appropriate to ask, chances are, it isn't. Curiosity is *not* a sufficient reason. Now, I do want to acknowledge your curiosity. Curiosity is okay, but you need to understand there are boundaries that are critical in business related settings.

One situation when it is okay to ask, and this might be scary as hell to fathom, is asking someone their preferred pronoun. At many LGBTQ events you will see nametags that have a place for a name, and then a spot for preferred pronoun. My nametag would say, "Hi my name is Jenn. My preferred pronoun is she/her." That way in a conversation someone knows to say she or her to avoid misstepping. Asking this simple question creates a safe environment for transgender and gender non-confirming people in the room.

Gender Non-Conformity "refers to behaviors and interests that fit outside of what we consider 'normal' for a child or adult's assigned biological sex. We think of these people as having interests that are more typical of the 'opposite' sex; in children, for example, a girl who insists on having short hair and prefers to play football with the boys, or a boy who wears dresses and wishes to be a princess. These are considered gender-variant or gender non-conforming behaviors and interests."[15]

When you attend an event that does not provide a place to note preferred pronouns, it is important to know how to handle the situation. The first thing you can do is make sure you know the name of the person you are speaking with and avoid using pronouns altogether. This can get clunky and awkward, but it is better than saying he when you should be saying she or vice versa. In the right setting it is completely acceptable for you to say "I'm sorry. Do you mind if I ask which pronoun you prefer?" It is possible the person might tell you that they prefer 'they' or 'zhe' rather than what you expected which would be 'she' or 'he.' The English language is evolving, as are we.

Let me share a story.

I was meeting with a colleague who had recently hired a young person who was very masculine in appearance. At the start of the job this person asked to be called Andy rather than their legal name. This person only stated they wanted to be called Andy and did not specify which pronoun to use. The challenge was that

---

15 http://www.genderdiversity.org/resources/terminology/#gendervariance

co-workers were using the requested name of Andy, but were saying she when a pronoun was needed.

Unfortunately, no one knew if they should be saying he or she, or even they. (The singular use of the pronoun 'they' was the 2015 word of the year.[16]) Rather than being disrespectful or feeling as if they were, co-workers were trying to avoid using a pronoun altogether.

This is an instance where the question, "What is your preferred pronoun?" would have come in handy. In this situation I advised my colleague that she should directly ask Andy the question. Asking this question is squarely in the proper context. Because this person asked to be called by another name, they would have understood and likely preferred that you ask for clarification. Since this person was so young, they may have been afraid to go the step further and declare which pronoun they prefer, or honestly, they may not have even thought about it, until the awkward encounters started.

> As an ally you need to know which questions to ask and which to avoid.

As an ally you need to know which questions to ask and which to avoid. Someone like Andy needs to know that it is okay to provide that added information to people in their workplace or other settings. It is a very delicate balancing act and requires a heightened amount of social intelligence to know the right timing and right language of things.

---

16 http://www.americandialect.org/2015-word-of-the-year-is-singular-they

I understand what I'm suggesting can be scary. Honestly there have been times when I've been intimidated when asking someone their preferred pronoun. But in every situation it has ended well. If you ask the question up front, you will avoid misgendering the person, which creates a whole lot of unnecessary awkwardness and embarrassment.

People within the LGBTQ community will be shocked that you, as an ally, knew that was the right thing to do in a given situation.

Dissecting Orientation, Identity & Expression

Furthering down the line of very fine differences within the LGBTQ community I offer the following terms; sexual orientation, gender identity, and gender expression.

Generally speaking, when I've been referring to the LGBTQ community, I'm namely speaking from the standpoint of sexual orientation, which is defined as—

"Sexual orientation is an enduring personal quality that inclines people to feel romantic or sexual attraction (or a combination of these) to persons of the opposite sex or gender, the same sex or gender, or to both sexes or more than one gender. These attractions are generally subsumed under heterosexuality, homosexuality, and bisexuality, while asexuality (the lack of romantic or sexual attraction to others) is sometimes identified as the fourth category."[17]

---

17 http://en.wikipedia.org/wiki/Sexual_orientation

Where the misunderstood nuance begins to unfold is when we define gender identity, which is defined as—

"Gender identity is a person's private sense, and subjective experience, of their own gender. This is generally described as one's private sense of being a man or a woman, consisting primarily of the acceptance of membership into a category of people: male or female. All societies have a set of gender categories that can serve as the basis of the formation of a social identity in relation to other members of society. In most societies, there is a basic division between gender attributes assigned to males and females. In all societies, however, some individuals do not identify with some (or all) of the aspects of gender that are assigned to their biological sex."[18]

Often you'll hear people trying to compare sexual orientation to gender identity, claiming they are the same thing, or using them interchangeably. As you can see from the definitions above this is not the case. Comparing sexual orientation to gender identity is like comparing apples and oranges. They're both fruit but that's where their similarities end.

If we look at how the LGBTQ community breaks out, it looks like this—

Lesbian, gay and bisexual all fall under sexual orientation. The commonality here is that sexual orientation is about the sex you are attracted to. For example; I am a female, attracted to other females, which makes me a lesbian. Or a male attracted to another male makes him gay. Or a male or female attracted to both males and females makes that person bisexual.

---

18 http://en.wikipedia.org/wiki/Gender_identity

Gender identity on the other hand has nothing to do with whom you are attracted to. It has to do with whom you identify as. I am a cisgender female (remember what that means?). I am someone who was biologically born female and identify as a female.

Now someone whose biological sex at birth was female but identifies as a male would be someone who is a transgender. The appropriate language would be a transgender man or trans man. The same holds true for someone whose biological sex at birth was male but who identifies as female. The appropriate language here would be a transgender woman or a trans woman.

Now, if someone is transgender that does not mean they are attracted to the same sex. A trans man could be straight, gay or bisexual. And a trans woman could be straight, lesbian or bisexual. The two have nothing to do with one another.

I understand this may be a lot of information to comprehend, so I encourage you to re-read this section if you need to. This content is critical to your understanding of the LGBTQ community.

Before you get too comfortable, I am going to throw the term gender identity at you.

Now just as sexual orientation and gender identity are like apples and oranges, two fruits—gender identity and gender expression are like comparing Granny Smith apples to McIntosh apples. They're both fruits, hell even both apples, but they're still different.

"Gender Expression is the range of physical, mental, and behavioral characteristics pertaining to, and differentiating between, masculinity and femininity. Depending on the context, the term may refer to biological sex (i.e. the state of being male, female or intersex), sex-based social structures (including gender roles and other social roles), or gender identity."[19]

What we've added to the equation is gender expression. Gender expression is the way you express your gender to society which can include the way you dress, the way you behave, mannerisms and appearance. The best way to describe everything is with a visual.

Now I'd like to introduce you to the Genderbread Person.[20] This diagram, in an oversimplified form, will show you how these terms relate to one another.

Sidebar: The Genderbread Person can be seen as controversial because of how simply it breaks things down. I fully recognize that this is a very basic description, but for the sake of this 101 discussion I am consciously choosing to use it as an educational tool.

19 http://en.wikipedia.org/wiki/Gender_expression

20 http://itspronouncedmetrosexual.com/genderbread-person/

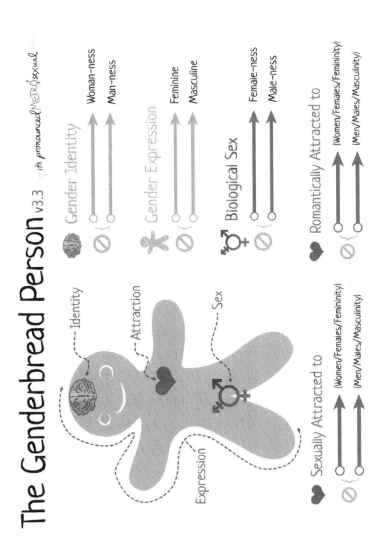

Created by Sam Killermann, TEDx Speaker
of "Understanding the Complexities of Gender."

Queer

Before we talk about what the Q most often means in LGBTQ, let's talk about an alternative meaning, questioning. Very simply it is "The *questioning* of one's gender, sexual identity, sexual orientation, or all three. It is a process of exploration by people who may be unsure, still exploring, and concerned about applying a social label to themselves for various reasons."[21]

Lastly, let's discuss the Q in LGBTQ, queer. The word queer is wrapped in a complex and misunderstood package. If nothing else understanding the nuance of queer is an imperative before you set out in your LGBTQ outreach. There are a lot of questions that surface around when or if you can use this word, and if so, in what context—Social? Business? Corporate?

This is not an easy answer. Let me share a story of a Fortune 100 corporation who reached out to me and eventually became a client. This is the email I received—

> *"Hi Jenn, I am the lead of X's Employee Resource Group. We are starting to look at the generational differences in our employees with LGBT. I want to use our internal social network to start a conversation around the word 'queer.' I know I'm a glutton for punishment. It's a word that is censored on our social network, and yet we have folks who are trying to reclaim the word. How can I frame a discussion around the subject knowing that people have very strong feelings about the word, but still accomplish our goal by bridging a possible generational gap about a word that in controversial yet*

---

21 https://en.wikipedia.org/wiki Questioning_(sexuality_and_gender)

evolving. Specifically, how would you frame the question? To me, just saying, 'What do you think of the word 'queer,' is just pouring gas on a smoldering fire. This conversation will be happening on our internal Facebook group. Would it be good to create guidelines and post them along with the question? I hope you don't mind the question but I wanted to solicit the opinion of someone who has more experience dealing with hard questions in conversations. Is considering this professional suicide? Thanks for any insights that you can give me. "

Wow, talk about a ton of hot button questions in one short paragraph! My answer to her is applicable regardless of whether you are in a corporate setting or you are the owner of a small business.

Queer is defined as "an umbrella term for sexual and gender minorities that are not heterosexual or not cisgender. Originally meaning 'strange' or 'peculiar,' queer came to be deployed pejoratively against those with same-sex desires or relationships in the late-19th century. Beginning in the late-1980s, queer scholars and activists began to reclaim the word to establish community and assert a politicized identity distinct from the gay political identity. Queer identities may be adopted by those who reject traditional gender identities and seek a broader, less conformist, and deliberately ambiguous alternative to the label LGBT."[22]

The most important takeaway is that the community is nowhere near consensus regarding the usage, meaning or implications of the word. If you stopped five people on a street and asked

---

22 http://en.wikipedia.org/wiki/Queer

them about this word, you would likely get five different answers, with a little bit of overlap.

When the term queer presents itself, there is a significant generational divide regarding the word and its meaning. If you talk with younger LGBTQ people (ages 33 and under), they often use the word queer as a term of empowerment. It is a word that they have grown up with and have come to embrace. With older LGBTQ people (ages 55 and up) the word queer was something that was used toward them in a derogatory way.

If you were to craft the same messaging toward LGBTQ people of all ages and use the word queer, you would likely find yourself with some not-so-happy customers. However, if you were strategic with your approach, you would understand that if you market a product or service to younger people, the word queer would be accepted, and in most cases, embraced. If you were to send that same marketing piece to an older segment, it would likely result in a negative response.

I haven't quite cracked the code when it comes to the folks that fall in the middle, between ages 34-54. It seems to be a mixed bag in terms of acceptance or rejection of the term queer. I advise those I work with to only use queer when they are targeting the younger demographic—to err on the side of caution. If you have a mixed age audience I would avoid using queer, at least for now. Maybe that will change over the next few years, but as it stands now, you are safer not using the word.

This is important for you to understand as it relates to LGBTQ outreach because there are significant generational differences that are worth being aware of. Marketing to an LGBTQ Baby Boomer will look very different from marketing to an

LGBTQ Millennial—be sure to stay mindful of this important point.

This chapter, in some instances, contains overly simplistic definitions. The intent is to provide you with knowledge to make better decisions around your communications efforts, not to downplay the reality or weight of these terms. I strongly encourage you to do further research on these topics, should you desire a greater understanding.

There are significant generational differences that are worth being aware of. Marketing to an LGBTQ Baby Boomer will look very different from marketing to an LGBTQ Millennial—be sure to stay mindful of this important point.

When you are fluent in basic terminology and have a higher level of sensitivity to certain situations, you are in a unique position to connect with the LGBTQ community. I can assure you that when you see something happening that shouldn't; when you gently educate someone on the difference between two related terms; or when you politely correct someone from using inappropriate language, your LGBTQ colleagues, customers and employees will be watching you with sincere gratitude.

CHAPTER 8

WALK A MILE IN LGBTQ LABELED SHOES

THERE ARE MANY variations to the expression 'to walk a mile in someone else's shoes.' While an old expression, I believe if you can put yourself in the shoes of an LGBTQ person for just one moment, you will gain clarity and insight that will help you fully understand the community in ways many cannot.

I'd like to start with the concept of labeling. One of *the* biggest mistakes I see over and over again is that companies and brands view the LGBTQ community as one large monolithic mass of people with one label, LGBTQ. They don't look beyond what might make someone who's lesbian, different than someone who's transgender. They believe everyone who is LGBTQ must look the same, act the same and shop the same. The reality couldn't be any further from this.

If you think about a potential audience for your product or service, chances are you do your homework first, right? You identify key demographics and psychographics to determine which markets to target. The same methodology should apply to the LGBTQ community. Simply being part of the LGBTQ community is not enough to begin an outreach campaign.

> One of *the* biggest mistakes I see over and over again is that companies and brands view the LGBTQ community as one large monolithic mass of people with one label, LGBTQ.

The LGBTQ community is truly a microcosm of a broader community in which people live and work. The community comes in all shapes, sizes, races, religions, and socioeconomic backgrounds.

Here's an example. If you're selling a spring break travel package, chances are your audience is under the age of 25 and undergraduate college students. If you advertise your LGBTQ spring break travel package in AARP magazine, a publication that is targeted to men and women over the age of 50, you would clearly miss the mark.

I've seen many organizations throw conventional wisdom out the window and treat the LGBTQ community as if no other common sense marketing or business principles apply.

Here's a personal example. My family of four lesbian household—I'm married with two children—received a piece of direct mail which featured shirtless gay men. Why? Because my wife and I are both coded in a database as LGBTQ.

Quite frankly we have nothing in common with 21-year-old gay men. Yes, we are both identified within the community, but the marketing message to me should be drastically different from the one targeted to the young, gay male audience.

Receiving this piece of direct mail tells me that this company is clueless about the LGBTQ community. Again, conventional wisdom applies. If your audience is primarily women, work with the LBTQ of the community. If your audience is men, work with the GBTQ of the community. Do not start selling your product or service to people who clearly fall outside of your target market—just because they all fall under the LGBTQ umbrella.

The best countermeasure to this misstep is to adopt an *Inclusion Based Marketing* approach, a phrase I coined many years ago when I was working in marketing. The idea is to create an *Inclusion Based Marketing* and communications plan, rather than creating separate plans for separate audiences. Instead of isolating a specific audience like LGBTQ people, companies are starting to include LGBTQ people in their mainstream advertising. Many companies, especially the big brands, have been using inclusion based marketing for years with strong results.

Mom First, Lesbian Second

As *the* Professional Lesbian I am often asked questions as it relates to reaching out to lesbians. Unfortunately, lesbians are not viewed as huge target markets to big advertisers. Often big brands will focus their energy on marketing to the cisgender gay man. This is certainly frustrating from my vantage point, but this by no means implies there isn't a vibrant lesbian community to work with. You just have to know how to authentically connect.

Sidebar: I was interviewed by BuzzFeed on this very topic.

The article is quite colorful! I've included the link in the references section.

I walked away from a discussion one day thinking, how could I, as *the* Professional Lesbian, reach more lesbians? Unable to come up with a definitive and clear answer I thought, well, if someone was trying to market to me, what would be their best approach?

Let me explain with a story.

A few years ago while traveling with my family to Lake George, New York I had an 'ah-hah' moment of sorts. Lake George is a quaint area in Upstate New York that attracts visitors from around the globe. My wife and I, along with our two children were playing tourists for the weekend. In our travels we passed a motel on the main stretch of road that had visibly hung a rainbow flag outside. I quickly pulled out my phone to search and see if this motel was outwardly marketing to the LGBTQ community—it was! The average passerby would never have known that the rainbow flag hanging outside the motel was a signal to the LGBTQ community that it is safe to stay here, but I noticed, and my wife noticed, which is all that matters.

Sidebar: Since the 1970s, the rainbow flag has been used as the symbol of LGBTQ pride. While hanging the flag of pride outside of your business, or hanging one virtually on your website or social media page sends a clear message to the LGBTQ community, I encourage you to implement strategies that go beyond this simple approach. In this post-Orlando, politically charged climate, it is imperative that members of the LGBTQ community and its allies move beyond it—*Beyond the Rainbow.*

At that moment it hit me—my family of four was traveling

simply as a family, not as a lesbian family. Being a lesbian couple didn't have any bearing on anything we were doing that day. We were a family seeking ways to entertain our children, not a lesbian family seeking ways to entertain our children—there is a significant difference.

The way to market to our family, in that moment, was by connecting with us as the parents of young children, not lesbian moms of young children. Our identities as lesbians came second to being mothers in this scenario.

This really got me thinking about those pesky labels we use to define ourselves.

Here's an interesting exercise. I want you to quickly write down eight ways in which you define yourself. Use the space provided to write your answer. There is no right or wrong answer. This is about you.

1. _____

_____

2. _____

_____

3. _____

_____

4. _____

_____

5. _____

_____

6. _____

_____

7. _____

_____

8. _____

_____

Now (if you are straight) is being heterosexual on your list? My guess is no. Most people, including LGBTQ people, are not walking around, looking through sexual identity tainted glasses. I developed the moniker of *THE* Professional Lesbian not because of who I am, nearly as much as it has to do with the consulting work I do and how I educate people for a living.

If I am being honest with myself, and with you, and look at the ways in which I define myself—being a lesbian is not at the top of my list, just like being straight is probably not on your list at all, let alone at the top of it.

Here are the top eight ways I define myself.

1. A woman

2. An entrepreneur

3. A wife

4. A mother

5. An advocate

6. An animal lover

7. A lesbian

8. A runner

As you can see, lesbian is toward the bottom of my list. If being part of the LGBTQ community is lower on my list and I am *THE* Professional Lesbian, imagine where it might land on lists for LGBTQ people who are not professionally 'out' for a living?

A Lesson in Contradictions & Lesbian Labels

I needed to lay the foundation on labels to essentially contradict what I just said to you. While being part of the LGBTQ community is low on the list of how I see myself and how I define myself, it by no means is something that isn't a factor in my every day life. What I am referring to is how 'out' an LGBTQ person is in their day-to-day life, with family, in social circles, and in the workplace. LGBTQ people fear for their safety. Every day there are opportunities to come out as LGBTQ or not to. This is emotionally exhausting.

The coming out process can be riddled with strife whether you are coming out to family members or friends or coming out in the workplace. Some people have a specific gender expression that sends a signal to people that they are likely part of the LGBTQ community, while others don't. When you have someone who 'looks the part' based on appearance, mannerisms, and stereotypes, it is easier to see them and market to them. As much as I don't like writing those words, there is truth to them, and I want this to book to be nothing but the honest truth even if it upsets some in the process. We are creating change together, here!

For every visible LGBTQ person you can outwardly reach, there are just as many, if not more, that are overlooked by the LGBTQ community and the straight community. This is where added nuance comes into play.

I shared with you the story of seeing the motel in Lake George displaying a rainbow flag and my family knowing that would be a safe place to stay, should we have needed to. In this particular example, our being LGBTQ was less important than our time together as a family. To some, our family could have been invisible as an LGBTQ family, we could have been 'flying under the radar.' When we look at two women in a relationship, they can often be passed off as sisters, best friends or cousins. When two women are on a trip together it isn't always assumed they are in a same-sex relationship. This is not the case, however, for gay men traveling in pairs. Sadly, people tend to be less forgiving of male couples than of female couples. It is a sad reality, but this is the reality nonetheless.

Some LGBTQ markets are more easily hidden, which is why being inclusive in your approach from a marketing or communications stand point is so crucial.

> Being inclusive in your approach from a marketing or communications stand point is crucial.

I recall when I first came out at age 19, I was young and naive. I didn't fit in to what people believed lesbians 'looked like.' It was very difficult for me to be openly and noticeably gay. Why does this matter? Because it's about living an authentic life and being who you are. If you don't 'look the part,' living authentically can be a bit difficult.

There is a whole culture of the LBTQ community of lesbians who identify as femmes, high femmes or lipstick lesbians—just to name a few of the terms. These are all women who do not fall into any preconceived stereotype of what a lesbian 'looks like' including short hair, having a rugged disposition or wearing more masculine clothing. While there are many lesbians who personify these stereotypes, there are just as many who do not. But you may not see, or notice them. They are invisible.

For some people belonging to a community is very important. For others it doesn't matter. Going back to when I was 19, I wanted to fit in with the LGBTQ community in order to find that sense of belonging. I remember wearing rainbow necklaces, sporting Human Rights Campaign jewelry, and I even wore a shirt that read 'I love my girlfriend.' Putting myself on display was how I tried to be recognized and accepted by a community that I was part of, but didn't easily fit in to. This is common among lesbians, or at least those I've spoken with. Which is why marketing to the lesbians of the community can be so difficult.

Even now, as out as I am as *the* Professional Lesbian, it occasionally happens where someone doesn't know I am part of the LGBTQ community and will make some kind of disparaging remark in my presence. A good example is a previous neighbor of mine. She was older, and the entire time we lived there, she was convinced that my wife and I were sisters. It was this way for seven years—even after correcting her it didn't make much of a difference.

My point here is, not only are many lesbians invisible to the broader community trying to market to them, but they are often times invisible within the LGBTQ community itself. This is why taking an *Inclusion Based Marketing* approach in all of your communications and messaging efforts is so important.

Open for (LGBTQ) Business

To be effective, you need to get a good grasp on the mindset of your potential LGBTQ consumer. The coming out process has a significant impact on how LGBTQ consumers do things.

Let me share a story to help illustrate what walking a mile in my shoes feels like.

When my wife and I were cleaning out our refrigerator, we dumped too many leftovers into the garbage disposal. This caused a significant plumbing issue. We immediately called a friend who's a plumber. He looked at it and couldn't fix it. He suggested we call another plumber who had different equipment.

I took to Facebook to ask friends for recommendations. Having run a chamber of commerce for as long as I did, you'd think I would be set on referrals! Friends of mine had referrals but they were in other areas of the state, not where we lived. So I took it to good ole' Google. This is where the story diverges based on whether or not you are part of the LGBTQ community. The average consumer would type in 'Plumbers Hartford Connecticut' or some variation thereof. But I began searching for 'LGBTQ-friendly plumbers Hartford' or 'gay-friendly plumbers

Hartford.' Much to my surprise *nothing* came up! There was no plumbing company currently seeking LGBTQ clientele in the greater Hartford area. This worried me.

I eventually called the plumber with the best website. When he rang the doorbell I panicked and thought "should I take down my wedding picture?"—the one that is hanging right in our front entrance.

As LGBTQ people you have *no* idea how someone entering your home is going to react to the fact that they've just entered a lesbian household. They are a stranger—you have no idea what their belief systems, politics, and religious affiliations are. As *the* Professional Lesbian, I was distraught over how could I, of all people, be thinking about hiding my identity in my own home?

The take away here is that there is *nothing* different about fixing a plumbing situation for my family of four, than it is for anyone else. Our families are not different. The same service is being provided. Lesbians use the same brand dishwashers as everyone else, lesbians do laundry like everyone else, and lesbians cook in their kitchens like everyone else.

The point here is that the service you are offering the LGBTQ community is not altered or modified in any way because you are serving LGBTQ people. The service is not the point. The point is that you know how to outwardly attract LGBTQ customers and provide safety, while treating them the same as you would any other customer. Truly, there is no difference.

What can be tricky about this situation, if you find yourself on the customer-facing side of this, is that it can be difficult to outwardly express your LGBTQ-friendly status quickly enough to diffuse any tensions. You have to make that impression before the customer picks up the phone to call you or sends the inquiry through the contact form of your website.

As a customer, had I found this same plumber and they had a footnote at the bottom of their website that stated, 'we proudly serve our diverse customers' it would signal to me that I could hedge my bets that this company is accepting. It is not a guarantee but often when a company makes a statement about diversity and being inclusive, they usually mean everyone, in my experience.

The plumber presenting himself at my door that day came in and did his job, as he should have. Our sexuality did not come up in conversation, nor should it. But it would have put me at ease knowing I had called him from a company that visibly (even if located in a footer) stated they were an inclusive company to do business with.

I would love nothing more than for our family to just be seen as a family, not identified by our sexual orientation. But due to our need to label, this is where we are as a society and where we will likely remain for sometime to come.

CHAPTER 9

WHAT ARE YOUR INTENTIONS?

I T IS IMPORTANT to understand why clearly communicating your intentions is so important. In order to successfully engage with the LGBTQ community, your words and your actions must be in alignment. Far too often there is a disconnect, a misalignment, between what an organization is saying in theory and what they are doing in practice.

The key to working with the LGBTQ community is to be aware of how you are (or are not) communicating with potential LGBTQ customers. I've seen countless companies waste a lot of money by spending a fortune developing visually stunning LGBTQ specific marketing pieces while failing to implement basic communications training among their staff.

> It is important to understand why clearly communicating your intentions is so important. In order to successfully engage with the LGBTQ community, your words and your actions must be in alignment.

It can take a significant amount of money and time to acquire a new customer, LGBTQ or otherwise, so when you finally get them to walk through your door, land on your website, or meet with you in person—you and your team *must* know how to treat that customer appropriately.

Why? Because LGBTQ people, including myself, are guarded. We live in constant fear of violence and rejection.

Here's what I mean:

Imagine you own a fictional hotel chain called Grace Hotels. You've designated a portion of your marketing budget for outreach to niche markets, including the LGBTQ community. Maybe you've read my first three books on developing a marketing plan and a communications strategy, or perhaps you've read my blog. You've gone through great lengths to ensure the LGBTQ community sees you as authentic and safe. You are in it for the right reasons, and you are committed to serving this market.

Your marketing plan follows an *Inclusion Based Marketing* approach. You've created visually effective print advertisements which convey you are a welcoming place for LGBTQ travelers. And you have a rainbow flag hanging at your front door. You are excited because you've just returned from a travel trade show and you realize there is a world of potential when it comes to increasing your LGBTQ market share!

Now its been a couple of weeks since you've launched your LGBTQ awareness campaign and you are starting to see results— you can't wait to find out how your first gay couple's stay was at Grace Hotels. The tension is building!

Now the moment of truth—James and Robert, a gay couple, begin their check-in process. They have expectations that you are going to be an LGBTQ-friendly destination. They've seen the advertisements, they've heard the owner (you) is sincere, and they feel safe because they saw the rainbow flag clearly displayed out front.

Upon check-in, your front desk person says, "Okay, James and Robert, I have you checked-in for a four night stay with two queen beds." To which James responds, "Our reservation was for just one king bed. We just need one bed."

The front desk person reacts in a judgmental manner and states, "But there are two of you, surely you need two beds." Now awkwardly, James states, "No, we really just need one bed. Robert is my husband."

Now the front desk person says, "Ohh, you have a gay lifestyle. I don't really agree with it but yes I can switch your reservation to one bed." James and Robert are now checked-in but not without feeling humiliated and frustrated while simply trying to settle in on the first night of their trip.

This brief exchange between your front desk person and your LGBTQ guests has caused significant damage to your reputation. Their experience and the expectation of their experience was completely misaligned.

All of the marketing dollars and planning that you've put into this endeavor are now irrelevant because your gay guests who just checked-in had a terrible experience. They were judged and humiliated by someone on your staff. This is not reflective of you, personally. But it is your problem. You can say YES we are doing this, I AM committed, and the LGBTQ community NEEDS me. But, if this message and that training does not trickle down to the employees on the front lines, this is the dreaded outcome. This happens *all of the time*. And it is completely avoidable.

In a single exchange riddled with assumptions, actions and unnecessary commentary by one single untrained employee, you have lost a customer for life. Sure that customer may not say anything while finishing their check-in to avoid a confrontation, but you can bet you will be getting an e-mail from this couple that explains how their experience did not live up to your brand's promise. Additionally, those LGBTQ customers will go online and leave honest reviews of your property. Their intent is not to shame you or your company, their intent is to protect future LGBTQ people from enduring the same experience. Their safety was threatened in a very simple exchange.

This is the LGBTQ community in action. We have each others backs when someone has a humiliating experience or has been discriminated against. Whether it is in the most overt way, or whether it is very subtle and unintended, the details don't matter, we'll sound the warning bells. I *do not* want this to happen to you.

Conversely, when an LGBTQ person has a wonderful experience by trained staff, word-of-mouth will spread in the most positive way. Within the LGBTQ community word-of-mouth is powerful. A study from Harris Interactive found that *78% of LGBT adults and their friends, family and relatives would switch to brands that are known to be LGBT-friendly.*[23]

I recognize that you may be so progressive on LGBTQ issues, that you may have read that thinking 'Would a front desk person overstep like that?' Yes they would, yes they have, and yes they will. I have dozens of real life examples from clients and friends who

---

23 http://communitymarketinginc.com/lgbt-research-practice/lgbt-research-downloads/

have stories like this—ranging from large hotel chains to small bed and breakfasts. It is quite a phenomenon that is causing organizations across the globe to lose business despite their very best intentions.

The bottom line? Untrained employees are a liability and a possible detriment to all of your LGBTQ outreach efforts.

The Power of the LGBTQ Dollar

The LGBTQ community is armed with vital information to help them decide who they will spend their money with. Often LGBTQ people are marginalized so they learned decades ago that the best way to make their collective voices heard was through their wallets.

> The LGBTQ community is armed with vital information to help them decide who they will spend their money with.

Back in 2006, when I first began researching the LGBTQ market, one of the first statistics I came across was that the LGBTQ community's buying power was $641 billion[24]. Ten years later in 2016, the buying power was $917 billion. The market opportunity is only increasing.[25]

Buying power is defined as "an assessment of an individual's

---

24 http://archive.fortune.com/2006/04/25/magazines/fortune/plugge-din_fortune/index.htm

25 http://www.nlgja.org/outnewswire/2016/07/20/americas-lgbt-2015-buying-power-estimated-at-917-billion/

or organization's disposable income regarded as conferring the power to make purchases."[26]

The LGBTQ market has an estimated buying power of $917 billion. You may be scratching your head (like I did when I first came across this number) and wondering how $917 billion compares to the buying power of other groups? Let me put it in perspective for you.

Let's look at the 2016 buying power figures for the top four niche segments, including LGBTQ:

- Hispanic Americans = $1.3 trillion[27]

- African Americans = $1.2 trillion[28]

- LGBTQ Americans = $917 billion[29]

- Asian Americans = $825 billion[30]

Now let's break down these numbers further. The following Hispanic American, African American and Asian American data was taken from 2016 census bureau[31] statistics.

---

26 http://www.businessdictionary.com/definition/buying-power.html

27 http://www.nielsen.com/us/en/insights/news/2016/hispanic-influence-reaches-new-heights-in-the-us.html

28 http://www.prnewswire.com/news-releases/packaged-facts-african-american-buying-power-tops-1-trillion-300332139.html

29 http://www.nlgja.org/outnewswire/2016/07/20/americas-lgbt-2015-buying-power-estimated-at-917-billion/

30 http://www.nielsen.com/us/en/insights/news/2016/asian-americans-are-expanding-their-footprint-and-making-an-impact.html

31 http://kff.org/other/state-indicator/distribution-by-raceethnicity/

- Hispanic Americans account for 18% of the population at 56.9 million people.

- African Americans account for 12% of the population at 39.3 million people.

- LGBTQ Americans account for 4.1% of the population at 10 million people.[32]

- Asian Americans account for 6% of the population at 17.8 million people.

If we calculate the buying power of each group proportionate to their respective population count, the numbers become very clear. While LGBTQ Americans have the smallest population size at 4.1% or 10 million people, they still have four times the buying power per person than Hispanic Americans and African Americans, and twice the buying power of Asian Americans. The smallest minority group has two to four times the buying power of their diverse counterparts.

> The LGBTQ community is a significant contributor to the U.S. economy and a serious market to connect with, when done properly.

The LGBTQ community is a significant contributor to the U.S. economy and a serious market to connect with, when done properly.

---

32 http://www.gallup.com/poll/201731/lgbt-identification-rises.aspx

The Connected Consumer

The two most important words you can remember during this process are—authenticity and transparency.

The LGBTQ consumer is hyper aware of what a company is or is not doing for their LGBTQ customers, LGBTQ employees, and the LGBTQ community at large. There are numerous resources that LGBTQ people can access in order to find out if a company is doing good for the LGBTQ community. In today's fast paced online environment, negative or positive word of mouth, particularly as it relates to LGBTQ practices and policies, spreads very quickly. You don't want to catch yourself in the crosshairs of a negative social media storm!

> In today's fast paced online environment, negative or positive word of mouth, particularly as it relates to LGBTQ practices and policies, spreads very quickly. You don't want to catch yourself in the crosshairs of a negative social media storm!

The LGBTQ community is ultra brand loyal, which is defined as a "consumer's commitment to repurchase or otherwise continue using the brand and can be demonstrated by repeated buying of a product or service, or other positive behaviors such as word of mouth advocacy."[33]

In addition to the previous statistic, which states that *78% of LGBT adults and their friends, family and relatives would switch to brands that are known to be LGBT-friendly,* there are three

---

33 http://en.wikipedia.org/wiki/Brand_loyalty

other significant stats, which come from Community Marketing Inc.'s research[34]—

- *69%* of LGBT people say their purchases would be influenced by a buyer's guide that shows which companies have positive workplace policies towards LGBT employees.

- *70%* of LGBT adults stated they would pay a premium for a product from a company that supports the LGBT community.

- *74%* of LGBT people are likely to consider brands that support non-profits/causes important to LGBT consumers.

The first bullet point is where the difference really comes into play.

This statistic proves that an LGBTQ person will choose *not* to shop with a brand who is known to be anti-LGBTQ or a talented LGBTQ individual will choose *not* to be employed by a known anti-LGBTQ business. The key differentiator of this community versus others, is that a public guide exists to help LGBTQ consumers evaluate organizations.

The HRC recognized early on that Corporate America was going to lead the charge for LGBTQ equality and as such needed a system to help provide these companies with specific goals and objectives. This system resulted in a consumer guide, called the *Buying for Workplace Equality Guide.*

---

34 http://communitymarketinginc.com/lgbt-research-practice/lgbt-research-downloads/

You may have seen the blue and yellow equal sign sticker on a car, you may yourself have one on your car already. But not everyone knows what the HRC does. I would like to share with you why this organization, and their rating system is so important to the LGBTQ community.

> *"The Human Rights Campaign and the Human Rights Campaign Foundation together serve as America's largest civil rights organization working to achieve LGBTQ equality. By inspiring and engaging individuals and communities, HRC strives to end discrimination against LGBTQ people and realize a world that achieves fundamental fairness and equality for all. The Human Rights Campaign envisions a world where lesbian, gay, bisexual, transgender and queer people are ensured equality and embraced as full members of society at home, at work and in every community."[35]*

This is a pretty powerful mission statement! A pioneer in the LGBTQ equality movement, they have been getting corporations to pay attention to their LGBTQ customers and employees for almost 20 years through the use of their Corporate Equality Index (CEI), which is the source for their consumer based *Buying for Workplace Equality Guide.*

Companies are asked to fill out a lengthy questionnaire that covers a wide range of topics—including their equal opportunity employment policies and the availability of employee resource groups. HRC gives the company four to six months to complete

---

35 http://www.hrc.org/hrc-story/mission-statement

the questionnaire. A company's score can range from a perfect 100 down to a -25. The data is then compiled into the consumer version.

The guide is designed to help an LGBTQ person or ally make shopping decisions based on a company's equal treatment of customers and employees. The guide is color coded with red, yellow and green. You can see clearly when you open the physical pocket guide or open the phone app, that green is a company you want to do business with versus red, which means steer clear.

Companies who treat the community right and fairly, are rewarded with increased business. The LGBTQ community is one of the few communities who have such a powerful tool that guides their purchasing decisions. This is why being authentic and transparent is so incredibly important in your LGBTQ outreach efforts.

Remember, 69% of LGBTQ people answered a survey stating they would be influenced by a guide such as this, which means LGBTQ consumers are looking to do business with companies in the green, and avoiding companies who are in the red. I refer to the CEI to determine where I spend my money for the largest decisions, like buying a home, to the smallest decisions like which cat food to purchase.

Being aware of this Index gives you an added advantage over your competition.

Over time companies change and improve, so a company could have a 15 and move their way eventually to a 100. This guide is capturing a point in time, so companies that rank low today might be higher in the next edition. This is progress in and of itself. Each year more companies participate in the CEI and are using it as a competitive advantage.

Many years ago when my son was about three-years-old he

asked "is that the mean store?" He asked this as we were passing a gas station that has been notoriously anti-LGBTQ, one in which he has never been. At the young age of three, we would *never* have said anything specific to him about a store being mean or not, but we have answered questions like "that store doesn't like our family, so we go to the store who does like us." These are tough conversations to have with a young child. He took what we said at face value and moved on. We have passed this gas station hundreds of times and driven out of our way to get gas where we know their policies protect their LGBTQ employee base.

It is important to note that as I am writing this, this company has risen to an 85 in the latest 2017 CEI. Since the CEI has existed they've been as low as -25. Companies can change. They won't be penalized forever for previous anti-LGBTQ policies, but it takes time and commitment to make consumers aware they've changed their policies.

When it comes to the LGBTQ community, the first company to enter the market in a genuine and authentic way will win the trust of the community first. While this particular company is now up to an 85, many of their competitors have been at 100 for years.

The disconnect here is between the company's objectives of wanting to do business in the LGBTQ market and the customer base understanding their past history of discriminatory practices. Just because the company now wants to be better toward the community, it doesn't mean they'll grab a piece of the LGBTQ market share—yet.

With this particular company, they outwardly hated the LGBTQ community for decades—denying proper benefits to same-sex couples, backing anti-LGBTQ legalization and utilizing improper hiring and firing practices related to the LGBTQ community. This is a *very different* scenario than a corporation who has a low score because either no one filled out the survey or because they were doing something in practice but didn't have the actual policies in place. While both of these yield lower scores, the perception between the two can be drastically different.

The disconnect becomes greater if this company were to run print and magazine advertisements that feature LGBTQ people. The untrained eye may think, 'Oh wow, I didn't know they supported the LGBTQ community.' While non-LGBTQ people might think the company is wonderful for LGBTQ people, the community will see right through it.

Decades of discrimination cannot be erased with one year of an improved score on the CEI. It is going to take them a while to earn the trust of the community. I look forward to seeing how this plays out over the next few years.

Internal Champions

Years ago I was hired by a publicly traded, Fortune insurance company with 16,000 employees in the US, Canada, UK and India. As part of their strategic marketing efforts they had two goals; (1) to equip them with the strategies and messaging they'd need to properly do business with the LGBTQ market and; (2) to help them improve their CEI score which was a 10 out of 100.

The challenge was that their marketing team, which was less than a dozen people out of 16,000, understood that in order to successfully, and authentically, do business with the LGBTQ market, that they needed to significantly improve their CEI score.

However, other key departments did not share their same sense of urgency.

We approached this in two ways. First, I conducted a series of focus groups with real estate agents, mortgage brokers and other related industry professionals from all over the country who are part of the LGBTQ community. Our conversations focused on one key question: *What are you looking for in an insurance company as it relates to the LGBTQ community?*

Second, after an aggressive lobbying campaign by the marketing team, I was retained by their HR department. Over six months we worked on the CEI questionnaire together. My realistic goal was to take the organization from a 10 to a 60.

However, I was surprised to learn that many of the policies required to receive a strong CEI score were already in place—just not officially documented. In cases where required policies, benefits or trainings did not exist, they were eager to implement them as quickly as possible or to craft a plan for ongoing implementation.

The end result is that in the 2017 CEI this company scored a 90! What an incredible improvement!

By officially implementing workplace protection policies, they are now protecting their approximately 500+ LGBTQ employees—at a time where 50% of the LGBTQ community lives in states where it is still legal to be fired for being part of the LGBTQ community.[36]

---

36 http://www.lgbtmap.org/equality-maps/non_discrimination_laws

I believe my work with this company can be summed up perfectly by the following quote:

"Never doubt that a small group of thoughtful, committed citizens can change the world; indeed, it's the only thing that ever has."

— Margaret Mead

My challenge to you is to take the first step by assessing the landscape of your company. Take an honest look at your treatment of your LGBTQ employees and the policies you have in place to protect them. If you begin to uncover elements you aren't happy with, start an open dialogue and identify how you can fix these problems. Being authentic and transparent about your challenges will only gain you more respect from the LGBTQ community. Don't be afraid of being vulnerable, as counter intuitive to business as that may sound. It will help you build loyalty and gain trust among your employees and within the community. If you own the business, you are in a great position to fix any inconsistencies quickly to ensure your LGBTQ customer gets the best possible experience.

> Don't be afraid of being vulnerable, as counter intuitive to business as that may sound. It will help you build loyalty and gain trust among your employees and within the community.

STANDING YOUR GROUND IN THE FACE OF ADVERSITY

YOU WILL FACE adversity as you get involved with the LGBTQ community. This is less of an 'if' and more of a 'when,' so I want you to be prepared. There are two types of scenarios I see play out regularly. The first is when people question your motives. This isn't fun, but we'll talk about it. The second is when you've misstepped and have to do some damage control.

The reality is for every ten LGBTQ people who think you are awesome and are thrilled that you are making an impact from an ally perspective, there is going to be that one person who is a total jerk, who will set out to undermine you and question your motives. The short answer is to pay no mind to this person, but having been there myself, I fully respect that this is easier said than done.

Earlier in this book we spent time talking about your *why*

and building the foundation of your knowledge. The next stage of your learning is knowing what to do in the face of adversity.

I have a super technical term for the people who will be a jerk to you—crank pots. You can thank my children for helping make that term part of my everyday vernacular. A crank pot by my definition is someone who is cranky in general and has decided to direct their crankiness toward you, whether it is warranted or not.

However, we aren't emotionless, so when someone says something nasty, please know, it likely has nothing to do with you. I'm sure you've heard this advice in a dozen different ways, but I want this to be crystal clear. I do not want one person being a crank pot to you and for that to entirely derail your outreach efforts. The world needs more people like you and less of the crank pots who are trying to tear us down.

I am by no means immune to crank pots. It happens routinely enough that I've realized their anger is rooted in insecurities, so I cannot waste valuable energy toward them. It's what we have to do to protect our sanity and our reputations.

Here's a personal example.

I was at an LGBTQ conference which I attend every year without exception. A few close colleagues came up to me and asked me about my relationship with someone, a gay man. I explained that it wasn't great and while we mutually disliked one another, I was always cordial and respectful. They proceeded to tell me that during the conference this person had been saying some pretty unprofessional things about me, and making quite a few accusations.

In a previous life I would have immediately been upset, wanted to know every gory detail, and stewed about it for days.

But instead, I said to them both, "Listen—if anyone in that room spends five minutes around me they'll know I'm sincere. If anyone spends five minutes around him, they will see that he is miserable and his entire MO (modus operandi) is to disparage others." (That is the definition of a crank pot.) I thanked them for bringing this to my attention and I promptly took subtle action to separate myself further from his line of fire.

In situations like these—no matter what you do—you will not win. People like this want to provoke you. They want to attack you. They want to bring people down with their sinking ship. Please allow my words to come to your mind when this happens. The situation is their issue. It has nothing to do with you!

You Can't Please Everyone

Here's another example. I received this message from a cranky lesbian in response to an e-mail I had sent about the launch of my second book:

> *"I don't at all understand or appreciate the thought that someone has to TEACH people to market or advertise to the LGBT community. The product is either good or it isn't. I find it insulting, manipulative, and capitalistic. BIG THUMBS DOWN—GROSS."*

I know this woman personally! We belong to several of the same networking organizations. Based on the tone of the e-mail it's clear that there is no changing her mind. If someone sends you an e-mail like this, please know this is on them and has *nothing* to do with you. The LGBTQ community wants to hear your voice in the marketplace.

For every crank pot you encounter there will be at least ten other LGBTQ people who will be grateful you are using your ally voice for good. Keep that in the back of your mind when you find yourself in a sticky situation. Don't give them the attention and be confident in your approach. Also, make sure you respond to their comments regardless of what forum they've sent it, private via e-mail or public on a Facebook post. A simple, "I'm sorry you feel that way and I wish you the best of luck" should suffice.

You have to hit it head on, neutralize the situation, and be genuine with your comments. You will encounter resistance, it is just the nature of the beast.

A Little Research Can Have a Big Impact

We've covered the first scenario to help you respond to adversity. The second scenario to prepare for is when you've made a blunder and need to get your message back on course.

One example of a blunder is understanding the fine line between being confident and so arrogant you get yourself into trouble. I want nothing more for you than to confidently walk into an LGBTQ event and make it known that you are there to serve the community in the most authentic way possible. Confidence is key and this is attainable. But I equally caution you from crossing that line into the land of arrogance. How you show up to an event is equally as important as what you say at that event.

I had an experience where I watched a woman (a straight ally) nearly throw down with a group of people over how many states had adopted marriage equality (this was pre-2015). She was hell bent on knowing she was right. My estimation is that she came into the event feeling like she had to prove herself, but she was off by two states. When you are armed with incorrect facts and are acting obnoxious about it, no one is going to respect that. That approach is not going to win you business in any setting.

There are some simple things you can do to make sure you are prepared. When you walk into an LGBTQ event, in your home state, or a state that you are visiting, do your best to be knowledgeable about the political, social, and cultural landscape.

You'll be able to hold your own in a conversation as it relates to your particular state. With the passage of same-sex marriage in 2015, there have been many other proposed anti-LGBTQ policies and laws popping up all over the country. If you can walk into a room and understand that there is a proposed bathroom bill in the state legislature right now, you are way ahead of many others. Understanding those local efforts is a huge boon to your credibility.

The Human Rights Campaign is a great resource when it comes to understanding LGBTQ discrimination on a state-by-state level. If you go to hrc.org/state_maps—you can click on an interactive map that allows you to search by policy or legal issue or generally by state. Doing this simple research will make you a credible resource and a great ally!

I'm Not a Lesbian!

The second example of a blunder is a bit more severe than arrogantly walking into a room with false information. I've told this story hundreds of times across the country, so I want you to think long and hard while reading this cautionary tale.

As the Professional Lesbian, and like any other business owner, I network quite a bit. I network both in and out of LGBTQ specific environments. This incident occurred at an LGBTQ specific networking event. Let's set the scene. Imagine yourself at an LGBTQ event that has a good crowd of people. The crowd is an even mix of LGBTQ people and straight allies. It's the perfect environment for a business owner who is taking the right approach to marketing to the LGBTQ community.

You find yourself in a conversation with a straight (woman) business owner and a gay (man) business owner, which is to be expected at a diverse networking event. During this conversation you hear the gay man ask the straight woman, "Have you heard about supplier diversity? You should look into getting your business certified as LGBTQ owned. You are a lesbian, right?"

I'm sure we can all agree at this point that making assumptions often backfires.

This gay man made an assumption that this straight woman was part of the LGBTQ community. In reality she was not. This is a simple mistake and shouldn't have been a big deal. I've seen this happen before; the person will politely correct them saying something like "Actually I'm an ally" or something to that effect.

I have a friend, who when asked '"Are you a lesbian?" enthusiastically exclaims "No, but thank you for asking!" This friend is a true definition of an ally to the community who is beyond joyful when someone mistakes her for being a lesbian at an LGBTQ event. This may be an extreme, but you get my point.

If someone mistakes you for being part of the community at an event, honestly, this is a really good thing. It means you are exuding a level of comfort and confidence in a room of people you are trying to serve. This is something to be proud of. Of course, you can then acknowledge that you aren't, but appreciate them thinking you are. It is a very easy conversation, there is no awkwardness needed—I promise!

Unfortunately that is not how this story plays out. Making assumptions whether someone is or is not part of the community is likely to turn ugly regardless of what side of it you are coming from. But in this particular incident, this woman had a very loud and visceral reaction to being called a lesbian.

How would you feel if you saw a straight woman unravel before your very eyes because someone thought she was a lesbian? Especially when the person making the assumption wasn't doing so in a negative way—in fact he was trying to help her grow her business!

This was truly an innocent mistake gone terribly awry.

This woman, who was previously thought to be an ally, began yelling quite loudly. Her key phrase was "How dare he call me a lesbian." She also exclaimed "'I've never been so offended in my life" many times.

Now imagine being an LGBTQ person in that room.

Not only was she yelling very loudly at the person who made the assumption, but she began walking up to *every* person in the room exclaiming "Can you believe Joe thought I am a lesbian?!

How dare he." She was so appalled that she could be perceived as a lesbian that she was throwing a tantrum and talking badly about Joe to everyone in the room. It got out of hand pretty fast. To watch a business owner in her fifties behave like that was embarrassing.

The end result for this particular woman wasn't positive. Her reputation was hit hard within the LGBTQ community. Many stopped doing business with her and never went back as a result of this, myself included.

I estimate she lost tens of thousands of dollars in sales as a result of this scene.

If something like this ever happens to you—you have two ways of responding. The first is understanding that people make mistakes and if you are assumed something you are not, it's not a travesty. Relax. Think of how many LGBTQ people live their lives every day with people assuming they are someone that they are not. Secondly, consider finding a new place to network. If you are not authentic or genuine in your approach to the LGBTQ community you are going to turn people off from doing business with you. If it bothers you so much to be associated with the LGBTQ community, or even worse have it be assumed you are a part of the LGBTQ community, this is not the right place for you.

> If you are not authentic or genuine in your approach to the LGBTQ community you are going to turn people off from doing business with you.

The Recovery

Even in extreme situations like this one, there is still a way to recover from it. Had the woman in the story realized how poorly she reacted and attempted to make amends she may have been able to save some face in the situation. Sometimes it is not how you act but how you recover from those overreactions.

One time I had shared this story as a case study to a room full of travel professionals. At the end of my presentation a brave woman stood up and asked, "*What do I do if I've already committed this faux pas and want to right the wrong?*"

It takes a brave person to stand in a room of their peers and admit to knowing they've screwed up and want to know how to fix it. Before I could answer the question, a woman in the crowd asked if she could address the concern. I happily obliged.

Her response was simple.

"*Own it.*"

That's it.

If you've committed a dreaded mistake, back up and apologize to the person you've offended. The woman in the audience explained it's one thing to make an assumption and be totally off base, but it's another to own it and apologize for it, right then in the moment.

Just own it.

We all make mistakes and even if you are a pro at this, you'll still slip and make a mistake. If you do, just own it, apologize and move on. The next step I would advise taking is to ask the person who you've offended how they would prefer you handle the situation in the future. Doing this is going to give you big kudos in this person's eyes.

Common decency goes a long way when working with the LGBTQ community.

Here are some simple steps to guide you—

- Be authentic.

- Be transparent.

- Let your guard down.

- Show your vulnerability.

- Admit when you are wrong.

- Apologize.

- Show empathy.

None of these items listed have any direct specificity to only the LGBTQ community. This goes for any group of people you are working with. Being able to put yourself in their shoes for just a moment and just being down to earth and real when something goes awry is the best approach for righting the wrong. You will leave the situation with respect, which is much better than the alternative scenario I just described. Next time you say something you shouldn't have—think of ways that you can bounce back from it and show your humanity.

Remember, deciding today that you are going to be an LGBTQ ally, doesn't mean you are going to be perfect tomorrow. It's a work in progress. But you have a lot of champions in your court that want you to succeed (me!), so keep at it and don't get discouraged.

CHAPTER 11

SUPPORTING THE LGBTQ COMMUNITY THROUGH TIMES OF TRAGEDY

O N THE MORNING of June 12, 2016 I broke.

I woke up to my Facebook and Twitter feeds all abuzz. It was about 7am, and I was drinking coffee before my family was awake, when I saw what happened from a friend. My entire world is LGBTQ and has been for a very long time, so naturally I knew many people personally affected by the shooting at Pulse nightclub in Orlando, Florida.

The shooting hit so incredibly close to home for all LGBTQ people: 49 lives taken, 53 injured and countless others directly impacted. This was at an LGBTQ nightclub, one of our 'safe spaces.'

What happened at Pulse caused a seismic shift in the community. Our safe place was decimated. I remember going to my first gay bar in my early twenties. It was the first time I walked into a bar where it was okay to be gay. I didn't have to pretend I was 'just friends' with my girlfriend. This is an experience that unless you've been on the outside, is really hard to explain. As an LGBTQ person we navigate life always feeling slightly out of place.

I spent Sunday in shock and was glued to the TV. On Wednesday night I was on a plane to Chicago for a corporate training. This was a training I had been working on for six months. My audience was the LGBTQ employee resource group of a Fortune 100 company.

Only a few days after feeling violated and heartbroken, I had to collect myself and deliver a training to 25 eager LGBTQ employees on how being out in your career can impact you positively. Talk about a tough topic given the circumstances.

While I sat at the airport on the eve of the training I couldn't help but see the irony. I was about to walk into a room of 25 LGBTQ people and tell them being gay is a good thing; when 49 people were just killed for that very reason.

The Orlando Massacre brought up discussions on LGBTQ rights to the public consciousness in a way that had never been done before. As I sat in the airport I felt anxious, I felt afraid, I felt unsafe. I poured my fear into my keyboard to distract myself while I waited for my connecting flight.

I shared these words privately with the women in my mastermind group. I had to get my feelings off my chest and I knew they would provide a safe place for my words to land.

I hadn't planned to share my words publicly, but they strongly encouraged me to do so. They felt people needed to hear the rawness of my emotions in order to better wrap their heads around the significance of Orlando. I couldn't and I didn't at the time. These words were about me. It was not my place to make Orlando about me. But as time passed, I realized Orlando was about me. In fact, it was and is about every single LGBTQ person.

I share with you, what I shared with them that Wednesday night from the airport. This is uncensored and unedited.

> It was not my place to make Orlando about me. But as time passed, I realized Orlando was about me. In fact, it was and is about every single LGBTQ person.

"As I sit in Dulles Airport on the eve of a corporate training, I cannot help but see the irony in the world around me.

I am headed to Chicago to train 25 LGBTQ leaders on how to be bold, how to be courageous, and how to use their power as LGBTQ individuals to do good in this world.

I am out every day. It's hard to remain hidden with a moniker of the 'Professional Lesbian.' I find myself in curious positions frequently having to explain to people what exactly a professional lesbian does—usually to an amused audience.

But today is different. The last four days have been different. There has been a seismic shift in our world, the LGBTQ world.

I've never once truly been in fear of my public safety. There have been times at large LGBTQ conferences where the fleeting thought of 'wow, someone could take out a lot of

LGBTQ people at once here' have crossed my mind. Likely a thought the average American doesn't think about when attending conferences.

But now it is different.

I began today in my home airport in Connecticut. And for the very first time I sat in gratitude for a reason I am embarrassed to admit. I am grateful today that I can pass for straight, that perhaps I don't fully look the stereotypical part of a lesbian.

Looking 'gay enough' is a struggle for many people and at times in the past for me as well.

But today I am grateful I am not masculine in appearance.

I am grateful that I am gender conforming.

I am grateful to be mistaken for straight.

I am grateful for my fellow passengers to ask about my husband.

This flies in the face of everything I believe in. Everything that I stand for.

But for the first time I can honestly say I am afraid to be gay in America.

I've been quoted in dozens of interviews and publications citing that I feel as if my wife and I live in a bubble. A bubble where being gay, for the most part, is okay. Living in a generally accepting and liberal state.

But today is different.

I look around at the many faces surrounding me in a

bustling airport and wonder what their stance is—what they believe to be true about LGBTQ people? Do they wish all gays were dead? Do they believe it is a sin and it is God's will that we all die?

One deranged man took the life of 49 gay Americans—and shattered the security of an entire community of people in one tragic night.

I've generally accepted the fact that there are plenty of people who hate me for my gay 'lifestyle.' They don't usually bother me. I don't pay them any energy.

But more people are appearing and voicing their hatred because it now feels socially acceptable to do. With pastors, ministers, governors and politicians voicing their opinion of how we reap what we sow and the death of those 49 innocent people was God's will.

In this aftermath there are more people standing up for LGBTQ equality than those who are against it. But it is those who are against LGBTQ equality that are dangerous. They are the ones heeding the calls by others to carry out God's will to take down more gays. They are the danger and we are in danger.

As I sit here and look around I wonder who would look at me differently, if I were more masculine? Who would call me names if I didn't fit my gender? Who would be upset if I were using the women's room?

These are things I don't have to think about on a day-to-day basis but so many people within the community do.

Today I am grateful that I don't have to worry about this.

That I don't have to worry about the gun toting anti-gay American seeking me out specifically. But I worry for everyone else. I worry for the safety of my community—my friends.

Today is different. Today I live with an extra layer of fear I previously did not carry.

The community will rise above. I will rise above. But this will take time. And today is not that day.

Today I live as a hypocrite; today I am covering my lesbian identity in exchange for protection, whether it is falsely assumed or otherwise.

But tomorrow I will stand in front of a room of 25 LGBTQ leaders who are looking for inspiration. Looking for someone to tell them that they can overcome Orlando. That we are better than this and they have the power as individual LGBTQ leaders to make a change and make a difference.

To be out. To be bold. To be brave."

I arrived in Chicago to deliver that training.

As we started the day I paused. I acknowledged my feelings, my fear, my hypocrisy and the irony of our situation. It was rough. Many of them had been in Chicago flying from the Orlando office. This corporation lost employees and family members of employees. Many were impacted directly and much harder than I was. They were all visibly grieving.

Multiple times during our training we were interrupted by management trying to get details on how this LGBTQ employee resource group was going to put the message out to their 50,000+ employees, to stand in solidarity for Orlando. It was inspiring and gut wrenching watching these employees determine how they were going to support their LGBTQ employees, allies and peers. The rainbow LGBTQ flag hung at half staff from their corporate headquarters declaring to all that their LGBTQ workforce was important.

That day, I felt at home with a family of strangers during a pivotal time in LGBTQ history. We were united in our grief together. It is an experience I will never forget.

An Ally's Response to Orlando

While you may not feel the exact same things I feel, or how anyone within the LGBTQ community feels, it is important to know that in times of crisis there are ways that you can speak out and show support. Even if all you can do is change your Facebook profile to the banner that says 'I stand with Orlando.' That is better than nothing and don't let anyone tell you differently.

In the days following Orlando my friend Liz Miller, from the CMO Council, reached out to ask what could she do in a post-Orlando world. She had been fielding requests from her audience, who are C-suite marketing executives, responsible for some of the top brands in the world. They wanted to know what they could do, how they as brands could respond. I provided her and her audience, with these simple tips—

- *Speak out.* It is important for companies to speak up and speak out about Orlando. The community is paying very close attention to what brands are saying or not saying during this time of grief. A simple acknowledgement will go a long way. A statement on a website, in social media or to direct clients or consumers who are part of the LGBTQ community is a signal that you are paying attention.

- *Engage in the conversation.* Pay attention to what consumers are saying about your brand as it relates to the LGBTQ community. Engage with your LGBTQ and allied employees in a meaningful way. Show them that you care and that your brand has a heart.

- *Donate.* If you have a product or service that you can donate to Equality Florida or another local organization, then do so. If you don't have something to donate, consider volunteering or empowering employees to volunteer. Find a way to make yourself and your brand present in the community that you are aiming to help. Convey your support in an authentic and genuine way.

- *Show support.* Even something small can show that you stand with the community. Many companies are showing their support by changing social media profiles to a rainbow, some are lighting up their office buildings, and others are participating in or sponsoring pride events. If there is a way you can show your support by way of the rainbow, then do so. During this time of crisis, the more rainbows the community sees, the better.

- *Get personal.* As individual marketers, take the brand hat off. Reach out to family, friends and colleagues who you know are part of the LGBTQ community and check in on them to see how they are.

While these words were specifically around LGBTQ community support in the wake of Orlando, these are relevant points in any time of crisis and go beyond support of just the LGBTQ community. You could apply these five points to any marginalized community. This is exactly how *Change Happens in Business.*

You are now equipped with my best tools and resources to understand the LGBTQ community in ways like never before. You now see that we must look *Beyond the Rainbow.* You *can* do this!

> You are now equipped with my best tools and resources to understand the LGBTQ community in ways like never before.

CHAPTER 12

WHERE DO WE GO FROM HERE?

THIS IS IT. This is *our* time. This is *your* time. This is the rallying cry.

At the time of publication we live in a politically fractured society. A society where we don't know if we are in a safe space or not, it doesn't matter if you are LGBTQ; this unsafe feeling is being felt by many.

This is it. This is *our* time. This is *your* time. This is the rallying cry.

The LGBTQ community has reason to feel unsafe, perhaps a little more than most. We are on the receiving end of hate and discrimination in all facets of our lives—from the religious freedom bills that are denying LGBTQ people service based on religious beliefs, to the 'bathroom bills' that are denying LGBTQ people access to use the proper restroom.

This has to end. But this is not the end. This is just the beginning.

This is *your* time to use your privilege—to affect change in your business or your workplace.

We know unequivocally that discrimination is bad for business.

We've seen the negative economic impact of hate and discrimination. And we've seen economic growth when people stand up and declare that they don't want their town, city, or state standing for discrimination; or losing money because of proposed non-inclusive legislation.

When this happens, businesses, corporations and individuals rally together and unify. This is your chance to unify. To impact the lives of those you employ; those you work with; and those you do business with.

The bottom line is that *Change Happens in Business.* Together we can make change that will impact the world for the better.

Use this knowledge wisely.

Do You 'Get It' Yet?

I do not want you walking away from this book overwhelmed. This doesn't have to be a big deal. You don't want to be *so* cautious that you feel like you are walking on eggshells around the LGBTQ community, that you are afraid to make a move. You just need to be conscious of what you are saying and what you are doing, continuing to read social cues, and putting your best foot forward.

If you follow the guidance in this book you are setting the expectation that someone from the LGBTQ community doesn't need to worry about who they are when they enter your business, show up for their first day of work or engage in a business transaction with you.

This is precisely why it is so important that your entire company be trained on how to effectively communicate to your LGBTQ customers and employees. Ultimately this is where so many companies and organizations fall short. They put a lot of time, effort and money into attracting their desired LGBTQ customer and as soon as an untrained employee opens their mouth with something negative, offensive or inappropriate, within moments they've reset the expectation of your business—something you've worked so hard to create.

I haven't sugar coated anything in this book, so let's face it— the LGBTQ community *is* skeptical. I do not speak on behalf of the entire LGBTQ community, far from it. But I do speak based on the information I have garnered from interacting with thousands of LGBTQ people, business owners and corporations over the last decade.

We are skeptical of those looking to do business with us. Our skepticism stems from fear—fear that the person or the company isn't really there to help us. Fear that they just want to pander to us because they've heard the alluring statistics. Fear that the safe experience claimed is disconnected from reality.

The people, businesses and organizations who are only doing this for the money often depart the scene as quickly as they arrived on it. Because of this, LGBTQ people have a solid way of sniffing out the long-term commitment versus the casual passerby. Any community has the right to be threatened by outsiders who haven't yet shown themselves to be honest, transparent, authentic or genuine.

Do you have an answer yet?

Have you found your '*Why?*'

Conclusion: Where Do *You* Go From Here?

This book has been written to provide you with the knowledge and confidence to be an awesome ally to the LGBTQ community. You are ready to step out into the LGBTQ community, and be the best damn ally you can and serve the community in a truly meaningful way. Be the safe and welcoming company or individual that the LGBTQ community is desperately looking to do business with and work for.

This book is your primer to ensure you are in the right headspace before you begin your LGBTQ outreach.

I recommend the following next steps:

1. Learn the nuanced language of what inappropriate questions, comments and/or statements you should avoid

2. Create a successful LGBTQ marketing strategy

Fortunately, I've written books on these subjects!

I encourage you to first pick up a copy of '*No, wait… You Do Look Gay: The 7 Mistakes Preventing You From Selling to the $830 Billion LGBT Market.*' Published in 2014, this book is a must read! It will teach you all the tips and tricks to avoid inappropriate or awkward communication with the LGBTQ community.

We just scratched the surface here and this entire book is focused on avoiding avoidable communication faux pas.

Next, I encourage you to pick up a copy of *'But You Don't Look Gay: The 6 Steps to Creating a Successful LGBT Marketing Strategy.'* This book is designed to take a very simple and measured approach to become active in your local (or national) LGBTQ markets. Released in 2013, the vast majority of the information is absolutely applicable to today's landscape.

You can download my electronic book, *'Marriage Equality Marketing: 5 Questions You Must Ask to Sell to the $917 Billion LGBT Market,'* released in 2015 after same-sex marriage became legal in the United States, for free at MarriageEqualityMarketing.com.

If you are interested in engaging with me in a more formal way, I accept consulting and speaking requests. If you are with a Fortune company with a low Human Rights Campaign CEI score, and are interested in how I can help your company get to a 100, please contact me. Additionally, if you are with a business or organization looking to hire a speaker you can visit my website for more information, JennTGrace.com.

The best way to stay up to date is to bookmark my website, JennTGrace.com. I've accumulated a lot of knowledge over the last decade and you'll find more than 400 articles and 100 podcast episodes archived here. This information is entirely free and will supplement what you've learned in this book.

You can also keep up with all my content by subscribing to my e-newsletter, *The Inner Circle.* I am conscious of your inbox and only e-mail about once a month. Head on over to jenntgrace.com/beyond-innercircle to sign up!

Finally, you can connect with me online. I am on a number of social media platforms and invite you to be part of my online network:

- Connect on Facebook at facebook.com/lgbtbusinessstrategist

- Connect on Twitter at twitter.com/jenntgrace

- Connect on LinkedIn at linkedin.com/in/jenntgrace

- Listen to the Podcast at jenntgrace.com/thepodcast

Lastly, if you are a purpose driven person, who has a story to tell and wants to do so in a more impactful way, check out my publishing house, Purpose Driven Publishing. Our mission it to make the world a better and safer place for all of us who live in it. Visit PurposeDrivenPublishing.com for more information.

As always, if you have a story to share, a question to ask, or have any comments, please e-mail me at jenn@jenntgrace.com.

GLOSSARY

Chapter Four

An Ally is "a heterosexual person who supports equal civil rights, gender equality, and LGBT social movements, and who challenges homophobia and transphobia. A straight ally believes that LGBT people face discrimination and thus are socially and economically disadvantaged. Straight allies aim to use their position as heterosexual and/or cisgender individuals in a society focused on heteronormativity to fight homophobia and transphobia."[37]

"Heteronormativity is the belief that people fall into distinct and complementary genders (man and woman) with natural roles in life. It assumes that heterosexuality is the only sexual orientation or only norm, and states that sexual and marital relations are most (or only) fitting between people of opposite sexes. Consequently, a 'heteronormative' view is one that involves alignment of biological sex, sexuality, gender identity and gender roles. Heteronormativity is often linked to heterosexism and homophobia."[38]

---

37 http://en.wikipedia.org/wiki/Straight_ally

38 https://en.wikipedia.org/wiki/Heteronormativity

"*Homophobia* encompasses a range of negative attitudes and feelings toward homosexuality or people who are identified or perceived as being lesbian, gay, bisexual or transgender (LGBT). It has been defined as contempt, prejudice, aversion, hatred or antipathy, may be based on irrational fear, and is often related to religious beliefs." [39]

"*Transphobia* is a range of negative attitudes and feelings toward transgender or transsexual people, or toward transsexuality. Transphobia can be emotional disgust, fear, anger or discomfort felt or expressed towards people who do not conform to society's gender expectations. It is often expressed alongside homophobic views and hence is often an aspect of homophobia. Transphobia is a type of prejudice and discrimination similar to racism and sexism, and transgender people of color are often subjected to all three forms of discrimination at once." [40]

An Advocate is "a person who speaks or writes in support or defense of a person, cause, etc. or a person who pleads for or in behalf of another; intercessor." [41]

Activism, in a "general sense, can be described as intentional action to bring about social change, political change, economic justice, or environmental well being. This action is in support of, or opposition to, one side of an often controversial argument. The word 'activism' is often used synonymously with protest or dissent, but activism can stem from any number of political orientations and take

---

39 https://en.wikipedia.org/wiki/Homophobia

40 https://en.wikipedia.org/wiki/Transphobia

41 http://www.dictionary.com/browse/advocate

a wide range of forms, from writing letters to newspapers or politicians, political campaigning, economic activism (such as boycotts or preferentially patronizing preferred businesses), rallies, blogging and street marches, strikes, both work stoppages and hunger strikes, or even guerrilla tactics."[42]

Chapter Five

Allyship is "an active, consistent, and arduous practice of unlearning and re-evaluating, in which a person of privilege seeks to operate in solidarity with a marginalized group of people—

- allyship is not an identity—it is a lifelong process of building relationships based on trust, consistency, and accountability with marginalized individuals and/or groups of people

- allyship is not self-defined—our work and our efforts must be recognized by the people we seek to ally ourselves with. It is important to be intentional in how we frame the work we do, i.e. we are showing support for…, we are showing our commitment to ending [a system of oppression] by…, we are using our privilege to help by…"[43]

---

42 https://en.wikipedia.org/wiki/Activism

43 https://theantioppressionnetwork.wordpress.com/allyship/

Chapter Seven

"*Gay* is a term that primarily refers to a homosexual person or the trait of being homosexual. In modern English, 'gay' has come to be used as an adjective and as a noun, referring to the people, especially to males, and the practices and cultures associated with homosexuality."[44]

"*Lesbian* is the term most widely used in the English language to describe sexual and romantic attraction between females. The word may be used as a noun to refer to women who identify themselves or who are characterized by others as having the primary attribute of female homosexuality, or as an adjective to describe characteristics of an object or activity related to female same-sex attraction."[45]

"*Bisexuality* is romantic attraction, sexual attraction or sexual behavior toward both males and females. The term is mainly used in the context of human attraction to denote romantic or sexual feelings toward both men and women. It may also be defined as encompassing romantic or sexual attraction to people of all gender identities or to a person irrespective of that person's biological sex or gender, which is sometimes termed pansexuality."[46]

"*Pansexuality or omnisexuality*, is sexual attraction, sexual desire, romantic love, or emotional attraction toward people of all gender identities and biological sexes. Self-identified pansexuals may consider pansexuality a sexual orientation,

---

44 http://en.wikipedia.org/wiki/Gay

45 http://en.wikipedia.org/wiki/Lesbian

46 http://en.wikipedia.org/wiki/Bisexual

and refer to themselves as gender-blind, asserting that gender and sex are insignificant or irrelevant in determining whether they will be sexually attracted to others."[47]

"*Asexuality* (or nonsexuality) is the lack of sexual attraction to anyone or low or absent interest in sexual activity. It may be considered the lack of a sexual orientation, or one of the four types thereof, alongside heterosexuality, homosexuality, and bisexuality. A study in 2004 placed the prevalence of asexuality at 1%."[48]

"*Intersex* is a variation in sex characteristics including chromosomes, gonads, and/or genitals that do not allow an individual to be distinctly identified as male or female. Intersex infants with ambiguous outer genitalia may be surgically 'corrected' to more easily fit into a socially accepted sex category. Others may opt, in adulthood, for surgical procedures in order to align their physical sex characteristics with their gender identity or the sex category to which they were assigned at birth. Some individuals may be raised as a certain sex (male or female) but then identify with another later in life, while others may not identify themselves as either exclusively female or exclusively male."[49]

"*Cisgender and cissexual* (often abbreviated to simply cis) describe related types of gender identity where an individual's self-perception of their gender matches the sex they were assigned at birth."

47 http://en.wikipedia.org/wiki/Pansexuality

48 http://en.wikipedia.org/wiki/Asexuality

49 http://en.wikipedia.org/wiki/Intersex

"*Cisgender* is a term that is used to describe a person who identifies as the gender they were assigned at birth. So you may be asking yourself, why do we need such a term? Well, it's because cisgender is a way to describe someone who is not transgender. It's a more correct way of saying non-transgender. Saying non-transgender makes an implication that being transgender is abnormal, whereas saying cisgender and transgender doesn't make any implications in either direction. They are simply two words with equal meanings co-existing together."[50]

"*Transgender* is of, relating to, or being a person who identifies with or expresses a gender identity that differs from the one which corresponds to the person's sex at birth."[51]

Gender Non-Conformity "refers to behaviors and interests that fit outside of what we consider 'normal' for a child or adult's assigned biological sex. We think of these people as having interests that are more typical of the 'opposite' sex; in children, for example, a girl who insists on having short hair and prefers to play football with the boys, or a boy who wears dresses and wishes to be a princess. These are considered gender-variant or gender non-conforming behaviors and interests. It should be noted that gender nonconformity is a term not typically applied to children who have only a brief, passing curiosity in trying out these behaviors or interests."[52]

"*Sexual orientation* is an enduring personal quality that

---

50 http://en.wikipedia.org/wiki/Cisgender

51 https://www.merriam-webster.com/dictionary/transgender

52 http://www.genderdiversity.org/resources/terminology/#gendervariance

inclines people to feel romantic or sexual attraction (or a combination of these) to persons of the opposite sex or gender, the same sex or gender, or to both sexes or more than one gender. These attractions are generally subsumed under heterosexuality, homosexuality, and bisexuality, while asexuality (the lack of romantic or sexual attraction to others) is sometimes identified as the fourth category."[53]

"*Gender identity* is a person's private sense, and subjective experience, of their own gender. This is generally described as one's private sense of being a man or a woman, consisting primarily of the acceptance of membership into a category of people: male or female. All societies have a set of gender categories that can serve as the basis of the formation of a social identity in relation to other members of society. In most societies, there is a basic division between gender attributes assigned to males and females. In all societies, however, some individuals do not identify with some (or all) of the aspects of gender that are assigned to their biological sex."[54]

"*Gender Expression* is the range of physical, mental, and behavioral characteristics pertaining to, and differentiating between, masculinity and femininity. Depending on the context, the term may refer to biological sex (i.e. the state of being male, female or intersex), sex-based social structures (including gender roles and other social roles), or gender identity."[55]

---

53 http://en.wikipedia.org/wiki/Sexual_orientation

54 http://en.wikipedia.org/wiki/Gender_identity

55 http://en.wikipedia.org/wiki/Gender_expression

"*Queer* is an umbrella term for sexual and gender minorities that are not heterosexual or not cisgender. Originally meaning 'strange' or 'peculiar', queer came to be deployed pejoratively against those with same-sex desires or relationships in the late-19th century. Beginning in the late-1980s, queer scholars and activists began to reclaim the word to establish community and assert a politicized identity distinct from the gay political identity. Queer identities may be adopted by those who reject traditional gender identities and seek a broader, less conformist, and deliberately ambiguous alternative to the label LGBT."[56]

"The *questioning* of one's gender, sexual identity, sexual orientation, or all three is a process of exploration by people who may be unsure, still exploring, and concerned about applying a social label to themselves for various reasons."[57]

Chapter Eight

Inclusion Based Marketing is the intentional act of creating one solid inclusive communications plan, rather than creating separate plans for separate audiences. Instead of isolating a specific audience like LGBTQ people, companies are starting to include LGBTQ people in their mainstream advertising. Many companies, especially the big brands, have been using inclusion based marketing for years with strong results.

---

56 http://en.wikipedia.org/wiki/Queer

57 https://en.wikipedia.org/wiki/Questioning_(sexuality_and_gender)

Chapter Nine

Buying Power is defined as "an assessment of an individual's or organization's disposable income regarded as conferring the power to make purchases."[58]

Brand Loyalty is defined as "consumer's commitment to repurchase or otherwise continue using the brand and can be demonstrated by repeated buying of a product or service, or other positive behaviors such as word of mouth advocacy."[59]

Chapter Ten

Crank Pot by my definition is someone who is cranky about something in general and they are directing their crankiness toward you, whether it is warranted or not. People who walk around with a chip on their shoulder are upset in general and sometimes you'll find yourself in their path.

---

58 http://www.businessdictionary.com/definition/buying-power.html

59 http://en.wikipedia.org/wiki/Brand_loyalty

RESOURCES

I have compiled a handful of helpful resources for you in this section. For easier access to an online version of these resources please visit: jenntgrace.com/beyond-resources

Chapter One

State-by-state LGBTQ discrimination laws
    lgbtmap.org/equality-maps/non_discrimination_laws

LGBTQ Population Size Data
    gallup.com/poll/201731/lgbt-identification-rises.aspx

Chapter Two

Community Marketing Inc.
    communitymarketinginc.com

Harris Interactive
    harrisinteractive.com

The Williams Institute at UCLA
    williamsinstitute.law.ucla.edu

National Gay & Lesbian Chamber of Commerce
    nglcc.org

Chapter Three

Jenn T. Grace blog posts
   jenntgrace.com/blog/organizedposts/

Jenn T. Grace podcast episodes
   jenntgrace.com/thepodcast

Chapter Four

Defense of Marriage Act (DOMA)
   glaad.org/marriage/doma

Human Rights Campaign
   hrc.org

Out & Equal Workplace Advocates
   outandequal.org

Additional LGBTQ Organizations you should know
   diversitybestpractices.com/
   news-articles/22-lgbt-organizations-you-need-know

Chapter Seven

Singular use they
   americandialect.org/2015-word-of-the-year-is-singular-they

The Genderbread Person
   itspronouncedmetrosexual.com/genderbread-person/

Chapter Eight

Attention, Advertisers: Lesbians Buy Stuff, Too
 buzzfeed.com/laurenstrapagiel/
 shut-up-and-take-my-gay-money

Chapter Nine

LGBTQ Research
 communitymarketinginc.com/lgbt-research-practice/
 lgbt-research-downloads/

LGBTQ-American Buying Power
 nlgja.org/outnewswire/2016/07/20/
 americas-lgbt-2015-buying-power-estimated-at-917-billion/

Hispanic-American Buying Power
 nielsen.com/us/en/insights/news/2016/hispanic-influence-
 reaches-new-heights-in-the-us.html

African-American Buying Power
 prnewswire.com/news-releases/packaged-facts-african-
 american-buying-power-tops-1-trillion-300332139.html

Asian-American Buying Power
 nielsen.com/us/en/insights/news/2016/asian-americans-are-
 expanding-their-footprint-and-making-an-impact.html

Population size by race and ethnicity
 kff.org/other/state-indicator/distribution-by-raceethnicity/

LGBTQ Population Size
 gallup.com/poll/201731/lgbt-identification-rises.aspx

All links were accurate at the time of publication, June 2017.

ABOUT THE AUTHOR

Jenn T. Grace is a nationally recognized business strategist, speaker and author specializing in the LGBTQ market. Guided by the mantra, *"change happens in business,"* Jenn believes social change happens first in the workplace before spilling over into mainstream society. She is an Amazon Best Selling author and has been featured in *Forbes, The Huffington Post, The Hartford Courant and CNBC.*

Passionate about helping people share their stories of adversity, Jenn is also the Founder of Purpose Driven Publishing and the Purpose Driven Authors' Academy. She holds a M.S. in Integrated Marketing Communications from Golden Gate

University and a B.S. in Communications from Salem State University. A marathon runner, animal lover and novice birder, she lives in Hartford, Connecticut with her wife Andrea and their two children. To connect with Jenn visit JennTGrace.com or PurposeDrivenPublishing.com.

OTHER TITLES BY THE AUTHOR

But You Don't Look Gay...
6 steps to Creating a Successful LGBT Marketing Strategy

Visit JennOnAmazon.com to get your copy!

No, Wait... You Do Look Gay!
The 7 Mistakes Preventing You From Selling
to the $830 Billion LGBT Market

Visit JennOnAmazon.com to get your copy!

Marriage Equality Marketing:
5 Questions You Must Ask to Sell to the
$917 Billion LGBTQ Market

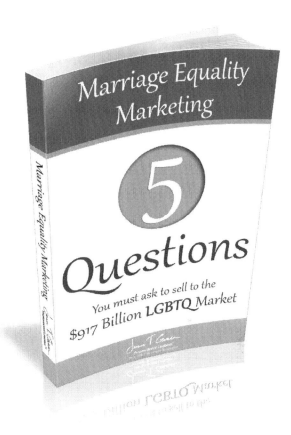

Visit MarriageEqualityMarketing.com for your free copy!

Made in the USA
Middletown, DE
02 June 2017